SILENT
PARTNER

SILENT PARTNER

A true story of life,
death, crime and surrender

BRIAN L. VIERS

Via Press
Chicago / Nashville / Tampa
2018

Cover Designed by Kostis Pavlou
Book Layout by Robin Black, Inspirio Design LLC

All Scripture quotations, unless otherwise indicated, are taken from the Holy Bible, New International Version®, NIV®. Copyright ©1973, 1978, 1984, 2011 by Biblica, Inc.™ Used by permission of Zondervan. All rights reserved worldwide. www.zondervan.com The "NIV" and "New International Version" are trademarks registered in the United States Patent and Trademark Office by Biblica, Inc.™

Special thanks to the Links Daily Devotional for the section on Perseverance. www.linksplayers.com

ISBN: 978-0-9996072-0-6

Printed in the USA

PRAISE FOR BRIAN VIERS/ *SILENT PARTNER*

Imagine being lost in the woods, needing to start a fire for survival and down to your last match. Brian Viers' story exemplifies this scenario. *Silent Partner* is an exceptional true story of survival and finding that direction.

—Tim Milner, President/ General Manager of Milner Broadcasting Company

Silent Partner is a must read and great gift for the soul. It will have a powerful impact on anyone questioning the coincidence in their own journey.

—Rick Selk, Executive Director, Youth for Christ Chicago

God gives all of us the opportunity to have a relationship with Him and gain the spiritual blessings that come with it. For some, the concept of faith is handed down in our upbringing, others have to read the signs God has carefully and strategically presented to them. Brian's remarkable story draws parallel to the latter and is an important testament as to how God can transform lives, if only the signs hidden in plain sight are recognized.

—Jeff Hammes, President/ CEO of Peoples Bank of Kankakee County

In this book, Brian Viers early years of trials and tribulations were filled with a spiritual hopelessness. His account moves through the people and circumstances offering change while proving nothing is impossible with his *Silent Partner*. The ultimate transformation in this heart-warming book is a wonderful account of God's patience, mercy and love.

—Matt Adamson, Professor at Olivet Nazarene University / Commander (Retired), Kankakee City Police

Be prepared! Brian Viers *Silent Partner* will change your life. His story of a reconstructed life is our story...in one way or another. You want answers? *Silent Partner* is The answer.

—Hope Hines, former Sports Director WTVF-TV Newschannel 5 Nashville, Tn. 2014 elected to the Tennessee Sports Hall of Fame.
Author: *In Hines' Sight, The Ups, Downs, and Rebounds of 40 years in Sports Broadcasting*

The youth I knew has become the remarkable man whose writing chronicles the journey he bravely undertook. *A Silent Partner* exist in each of us, but too often is not embraced. Brian's story explains the importance of allowing the Partner to be his ultimate guide through life. I am proud to have known Brian through those teenage years and today as he boldly moves forward with his all important *Partner*.

—Joseph Beard, Chief of Police Bourbonnais, Illinois 1979-2010

SILENT PARTNER

I want to give a special heartfelt thanks to a large number of people who not only believed and encouraged me over the years, but also those who took time to read and critique samples. To those who refreshed my memories and shared important details I had overlooked. I apologize now too for anyone I forgot to mention. Please forgive me as I am reflecting over several decades.

In the beginning I sat with friends on numerous occasions weeding through piles of notebooks. Yes, I had actually hand written every word I intended to include, mostly onto spiral notepads. In today's world it's a rarity but still a method of efficiency as well. Eventually I compiled a working outline. From there I began my quest for gathering details and expanding this material. Breaking down the process in this manner enabled me to drift in and out of sessions only as I felt drawn to work. Hence, several decades. Stories unraveled in my mind over time and only when the time was right did I commit them to paper. My manuscript still needed professional help. It was after a lunch meeting in Brentwood, Tennessee that Stan Moser offered up an idea. Having recently retired from a career at Word Records, he along with a friend,

Ed Chinn, brought his story to life in form of a book, *We Will Stand, Celebrating 40 Years of Contemporary Christian Music.* After reaching out to Ed Chinn, he agreed and reworked my material into a story. Bringing his extensive resume, he was a great help simplifying the process while maintaining my intended message. And then I waited.

Time, as I had relied on to this point, would soon open the door for print. After a round of golf at the Governors Club in Nashville, I had dinner with a new friend. Mike Arrington had recently retired as Vice President of Lifeway Christian Stores based in Nashville. Lifeway also owned B & H Publishing Group. He offered insight, as well as to connect me with another friend, David Shepherd, who was another recent retiree from their organization. David had been their Vice President of B & H Publishing. Time definitely proved to be on my side as industry experts had come out of the woodwork to assist on my project. I am grateful to each of these men for their professional input and assistance. David suggested a few additional changes and enter Greg Webster. He is an independent writer that many of the largest publishers use for his crafted skills and knowledge of the written word. Greg further twisted and turned parts of my story on its head. Often we went back and forth until materials hit their mark. This waiting period allowed the necessary timeline to unfold and bring clarity to my story. As I have discovered; It takes an army. Even the seemingly insignificant connections and events played a part in the bigger picture. Without help and the now friendships formed, I may still be waiting for the right time.

Let us not become weary in doing good,
for at the proper time we will
reap a harvest if we do not give up.

Galatians 6:9 (NIV)

To my wife Sharon,
a special thanks just for being you.
With Love

CONTENTS

Before I formed you in the womb I knew you,
before you were born I set you apart;
I appointed you as a prophet to the nations.

Jeremiah 1:5 (NIV)

PROLOGUE

In one motion, I threw off the bedcovers and jerked upright from sleep, body pulsating with each thump of my heart. Uncovered from the waist up in the darkness, I felt the December chill of northern Illinois even inside the house. Perhaps I had turned the heat too low before bedtime. But the mundane thought about temperature competed with a far more serious concern: *What startled me from such a sound sleep?*

Breathing heavily, I sat motionless in bed, trying to discern whether or not I was in danger. Shades drawn, the only light in the room glowed from numerals on my digital clock. I squinted toward the glimmer of red. *My God,* I thought, *it's not danger. It's the time!*

Pitching covers to the far end of the bed, I planted my right foot on the floor, but my left caught in the blanket. I lost my balance, fell onto my hands, and rolled several feet across the carpet. As I scrambled to get up, a panicked first step landed my right foot in a partially unpacked suitcase I had dropped in the middle of the bedroom. I twirled to avoid falling over an open box of stereo components and pulled myself upright on the bedroom doorframe.

In two steps, I crossed the hall and grabbed the stair railing. Using it for support, I descended three steps at a time, half-sliding, half-running to the bottom. I slapped the air until my hands found the table by the laundry room.

"Where the heck are they?" I hollered at the cold gloom around me.

I knew I had set out a pressed pair of black pants and button-down shirt for the church service tomorrow—no, today! But the clothes were gone!

I live alone. Who could have taken them?

Panic rising, I bolted back upstairs. At the door of my bedroom, I stopped, slid my right hand slowly up the doorframe, and for the first time since waking, coherent thoughts seeped into my brain. *The clock. Why am I worried about being late? It's only 4:15 in the morning.* I felt like the butt of a joke on a reality TV show. *And church? What am I thinking? I don't even go to church! What would I do that for?*

It still hadn't occurred to me to switch on a light, so I turned and plodded slowly downstairs in the dark. Where had these strange thoughts about going to church come from? Shuffling into my living room, I reached for the end-table lamp, flicked it on, and flopped across the couch.

The clarity of thinking about how ridiculous I was to worry about being late for *anything* at four in the morning gave way once again to mental gibberish. Passages from the book a friend gave me about God that I'd read in spite of my own better judgment rambled through my thoughts. *Forgiven? Relationship with God?* Then the insane—I assumed that's what it was—encounter with . . . an angel? The evening sky whose kaleidoscope of colors seemed to mean something? None of it made sense. *This must be what a mental breakdown feels like.* I stared at the lampshade by the arm of the sofa, and then tightly squeezed my eyes shut. Please go away!

I sat in silence for several minutes, hearing only the hum of the refrigerator from the kitchen. Slowly I relaxed my closed eyes and placed my face in my hands. *Yes. I know.*

I cleared my throat.

"I give up," I said out loud. As best I knew, I was talking to God and had only one thing to say to Him: "You win."

Chapter 1

CUTTING THROUGH THE SILENCE

A dozen screams erupted from the den as glass shattered against fireplace bricks. From my seat on the couch in the living room, I couldn't see the table-lamp-turned-weapon that "one of the guys" had pressed into use to defend himself against his attacker. Several male voices swore above the shrieks from girls as something like 60 teenagers pressed through the front door.

I wrapped both hands tight around my Miller Lite bottle, as if it needed protection from the chaos in the next room. The broken lamp had extinguished the only artificial light in the room. Now only the moonlight flooding through the bay window offered up any sense of clarity for the ensuing commotion. I laughed off the unknown hysteria but only momentarily.

Movement from the direction of the den cut short my amusement. A large male silhouette rushed *at me*. Moonlight flashed on the outstretched blade of his knife.

I jumped up from the couch and whirled away from the attacker, but not soon enough to completely avoid his first swipe. I winced at a searing pain across my lower back. Instinctively, I spun around and lashed out with my arms to protect my torso.

I dodged his thrust but lost my balance. Rough carpet burned my right elbow as I slid beside the couch. Fear poured the will to fight into every undamaged part of my body, and I scrambled into a defensive position as my attacker dropped toward me. This made no sense. I was thinking, "I know him!" Duane was a fellow wrestler on our high school team. Instinctively, I pushed hard off the floor with my right hand, then with clenched fist made solid contact with what appeared to be his chin.

He stumbled backwards several steps. For an instant, his wide eyes locked with mine. Is he crazy? What drugs had he done tonight that caused *this*? He slashed his knife past my face three more times but seemed less intent on doing damage. Duane let out a low growl and sneered at me before retreating. I held my arm for a moment before turning toward my buddy Rich who was now under attack on the other side of the room, near the end of couch.

Out of the corner of my eye, I saw Rich fall onto the couch.

From a seated position, he was trying to kick Duane away. Time stood still. The blood streaming out of my left arm distracted me from intently watching the nearby conflict. I heard Rich yell as the two young men scuffled in the dark, and I heard guys outside shouting obscenities over the sobbing of terrified girls. I knelt on the floor. Breathing heavily, I glanced up as Duane plunged his knife one last time toward Rich's upper body and then stumbled over furniture as he ran to the front door. A new round of screams erupted from the front yard as Duane exited the house and leaped from the porch and dashed up the street.

I straightened up and fell toward the exit. A half of dozen teenage girls gasped as I staggered out the front door, shirt drenched in my own blood. In the gray moonlight, I could make out five or six kids lying on the ground. I suspected they were victims from the initial melee in the den.

From shock, loss of blood, and maybe a few too many beers, I stood swaying at the edge of the porch looking to gather my thoughts. What just happened? A few feet to my left, steps descended to the yard, but I wondered if I could make it that far without toppling off the raised surface. I took a step, stopped to keep my balance, and then stumbled down into the yard.

As I tottered on the curb side of the street, the whine of police sirens roused my attention. *I'm hurt. I need help.* I sat down on the curb to rest momentarily. The slow movement of a car passing in the street recaptured my attention. I knew the car and recognized two female friends inside.

I yelled at them to stop. Lurching up toward the tan Ford Escort, I shouted at them, "Get me to the hospital—now!"

Speechless, the driver stopped the car, jumped out, and opened the back door as her friend rounded the car to help. Two girls bundled me into the back seat, and within seconds, the small-car-turned-ambulance rocketed down the street toward Riverside Hospital in Kankakee.

I lay on the back seat, blood from my left arm dripping steadily onto the floorboard. The damage I could see worried me, but searing pain in my lower back occupied most of my thoughts, and the haze returned. Reaching back to the worrisome spot, I discovered two holes just above my belt line on the left side. Panic set in. I began to share the facts with my drivers, possibly offering the smoking gun evidence to the would be case, which came in form of a fillet knife. Sirens rang out louder as additional units arrived. While the police scanned the area helping victims and gathering information I was being wisked away. *Am I going to die?* I was riddled with stab wounds. *I've never had a day like this. I'll remember April 28, 1990 forever* was my only coherent thought. The short five-mile trip to the hospital felt like fifty.

Our arrival at the emergency room revived my focus and stirred some hope that I might survive. My two caretakers helped me into the dead calm of the medical facility.

"Hello!" I mustered the energy to shout at the empty hallways. "Where is everyone?"

A noise from behind a service counter caught our attention as a lone receptionist shuffled out of a back room. Indifferent to my blood-soaked clothes, she slid an intake form onto the counter and began asking questions. Although I wondered seriously if I might bleed to death before she finished the interrogation. Anger at her lack of concern wouldn't allow me enough focus to complete the bureaucratic interview. Instead I demanded help. Now! She quickly obliged, either from my child-like tantrum or the decision to lie down and rest in the middle of reception area, making a bloody mess of the white marble floor. I was quickly scooped up and wheeled in for further interrogation by the physician. I wasn't much for conversation.

Once in a treatment room, a calm-faced forty-something doctor discovered two slashes and six puncture holes. One had gone completely through the thickest part of my left fore-arm, slicing between the radius and ulna bones. After jab-bing me with a few shots to numb the pain, he laced together my wounds as nonchalantly as if he were tying a shoe.

Ninety minutes after I had arrived at the hospital, an attendant helped me into a wheelchair and rolled my ban-daged body to the waiting room. My mother's sleepy, tearful eyes greeted me.

Now I'm going to hear about it, I thought.

Mom walked beside me as the medical assistant wheeled me to her car. She forced a smile and said only, "God must not want you right now. I guess it wasn't your time to go."

She made an attempt to defuse the nervous concerns, say-ing something about a cat, and nine lives, and something about me already exceeding that number. My thoughts had momentarily reverted back to her previous statement; *God must not want you right now.*

That struck me as an odd notion the night my mom drove me, left forearm still throbbing in pain, home from the hospital. When had God *ever* wanted me? And if somehow He happened to, it sure wasn't obvious to me. And what about the other kids at the party. Six others had been hurt. I guess God didn't want them, either. But by my mother's logic, the Almighty Whoever must have wanted Rich. He had only three stab wounds to my seven (the most of any victim that night), but the knife had penetrated his leg once and his heart twice, and he died. Maybe God kind of wanted the others but changed His mind. They were all in much worse condition than I was—two friends, Corey and Jimmy needed significant colon surgery—but they and the others all ended up pulling through.

So was that it? If God wants you, you die; if He doesn't, you live? The formula seemed dumbly simplistic to me, but it was all I could make of my mother's assertion.

To hear local radio reports—and see the Chicago TV news—you would think the Saint Valentine's Day massacre had occurred again in the quiet Bourbonnais neighborhood that April night in 1990. Al Capone famously slaughtered six members of an Irish gang from the north-side to shore up the gangster's control from the south of Chicago's multi-headed Prohibition Era crime business. Yet our south-side melee was simply a group of wasted teenagers with nothing better to do than cause serious trouble for ourselves.

Still, I wondered why I passed through the shredder that night with no lasting injuries (survivors typically ponder such thoughts). Like a sonar ping from some unfathomable depth my mother's observation wouldn't leave me.

At the time, meaningful reflection seemed like the right thing to do, but I had no idea how to do it. The best I could come up with was to think back on my life so far. Perhaps my long-standing penchant to fight had set me up for the fracas that ended in a fillet of my left arm and lower back.

As a boy, I drew strength from neighborhood fights. Nothing serious, they were more for establishing ground so as not to be bowled over I guess. In the subdivision Quail Hollow, a newly developed area in east Bradley the older boys routinely reminded us of our youth—like a sport. In a way we learned to take care of ourselves. But I also learned the value of fighting (or so I thought) from watching movie heroes like Sylvester Stallone. Rocky defied every bookmakers' odds and won his fights (well, *almost* won the first time). He didn't think much about anything deeper than how to train, fight, and beat up whatever guy stepped in the boxing ring with him.

Then Stallone became Rambo, and I thought he was even better. What could be more cool than a one-man army who could wipe out any battalion that came after him?

My depth of life analysis ended with an image of Rambo in my head, and I liked that. As a young man searching for an identity, maybe I wanted to be Rambo. Yes. *Perhaps I should put my love of action fighting to good use.* The only alternative I could see in my small Illinois town would end up with more nights like I had just escaped—but next time it might be me with two wounds to the heart, instead of Rich. So after high school, I joined the infantry.

Chapter 2

HERE I GO AGAIN

It's strange that doing something different so often seems like a solution to whatever problems we might be facing. The change may be unrelated to the issue at hand, yet we somehow think it will provide relief, renewal, revival, or the happiness that eludes us in our present circumstances. That hope certainly was in play for me when I took off to express my "inner Rambo." One phrase I discovered and continue to adhere to is: "Wherever you go, you bring YOU with you."

The Arrival

Late. My introduction to the Army's "hurry up and wait" doctrine came in the form of AWOL transportation to Ft.

Benning, Georgia. The Greyhound bus enlisted to take new recruits to basic training hadn't arrived, leaving a handful of guys about my age stranded at the world's busiest airport. At least instructions from my recruiter had led me to the designated staging area where, I assumed, someone would get us whenever the Army decided the time was right.

I slumped into a seat and stared at the humanity swirling around the interior of Atlanta's Hartsfield International Airport, entertaining myself by scanning the crowd. We joked while rating the women who passed by. The summer parties and part-time jobs kept my social network intact throughout and the Fall and into early winter, right up until the frigid afternoon I boarded a Delta Airlines 757 at Chicago O'Hare. That was barely two hours ago, and now my stomach churned at the thought of what may lay in store for me. Trying to keep my thoughts positive, I would hope for warmer weather at Ft. Benning, eight hundred miles south of the Windy City.

Summer had been like the rest of my life so far: warm and familiar. I wished I could go back to hanging out with the guys and girls, drinking beer. Not a care in the world. But there was no back door. I could only move forward. However bad my new world might be, though, I had one comrade on the uncharted path with me. My high school buddy, Jim Delong, who was among the fraternity of friends wounded in the stabbing fest the night Rich was killed. Jim and I joined the Illinois Army National Guard together and signed up for the same MOS (Military Occupational Specialty, the first of countless abbreviations I would learn for Army assignments, activities, attack plans, and weaponry). Now waylaid together in Atlanta, we were headed for the Eleventh Infantry Battalion (11 Bravo), and assuming our bus eventually arrived, would spend the better part of the next six months in South Georgia for basic training and AIT (Advanced Individual Training).

My thoughts still drifting through recent days that had suddenly become "old times," loud voices roused me to the present. When an overbearing male somewhere nearby screamed, "Viers!" I jumped, aware again of my surroundings. Mine was one of a half dozen last names barked rapid-fire by an enormous man decked out in camo and wearing spit-shined black boots. *This must be a drill sergeant,* I chuckled to myself. It would be the last time I took a drill sergeant lightly.

The man who had yelled my name thundered toward the staging area, followed by three other uniformed hulks. Hairs on the back of my neck prickled. Each steely face announced a new reality to the dumbfounded recruits: "We own you now!"

As the other greenhorns sprang to their feet, I realized I had also been formulating an exit strategy from what now appeared an inescapable fate. Reluctant to yield my civilian ground too easily, I slowly straightened in my chair, placed hands on my knees, and stretched lazily to my full stature, which left the top of my head just over shoulder height to the man who had called my name. It was also the last time I would do much of anything slowly for the next half a year.

The onslaught of drill sergeants was our cue that the Greyhound bus had arrived, and occupants of the staging area obeyed the first orders from our new masters: we formed a line. Suddenly, I could feel the bemused eyes of unencumbered travelers who had stopped momentarily to make room for the soldiers. Perhaps on a future day, some of them would thank me for my service, but tonight at Atlanta's international airport, they just stared. Audience watching, a half-dozen travelers, plucked from the ranks of those free to go and do as they pleased, trooped robot-like out the door.

Half the seats on the bus already held young male bodies, some still wide-eyed from their first encounter with the sergeants, others rigid and tight-lipped, a few struggling to look cool despite the hopelessness of remaining so under the tyranny of the non-com officers set on making us miserable for as long as they had charge of us. How the bus managed to be late for the evening arrivals, I could not understand once I learned the Greyhound had been circling the airport since mid-morning, picking up recruits from the various baggage claim areas. A handful of newbies had been on board for three hours.

We rode in silence—not by choice but by command of the sergeants—for two hours down I-85, then the road to Columbus, Georgia and on to Fort Benning. Most of the ride, it seemed, took place on the base itself. Our arrival at the entrance of the largest infantry training facility in the United States did not mean we had arrived. Late afternoon sun cast exaggerated shadows from the fifty-foot tall pine trees dashing past the bus window. I stared at the woods that looked more like a state park than an Army base until the trees gave

way to wide stretches of flat, grassy land. Soldiers in formation spread across the open spaces. As the bus rocked past
them, I watched, incredulous, as countless human machines
marched in perfect rows and columns. Over the rumble of
the bus, I could hear hundreds of hardy voices sounding off
in cadence.

Once off the bus, I could see the thought in the eyes of
most of my fellow recruits: *Don't you even think of messing with
me.* Testosterone ran high for the first several days of Basic,
but "the look" merely camouflaged the insecurity of 18- and
19-year-old males whose identities had been ripped away
from them. Baffled by our new life in uniform, we walked
and talked tough as a survival technique. Obviously, the drill
sergeants had seen it all before, yet we had to cycle through
the process of getting ground into teachable, drillable, obedi-
ent fighters.

In just three days, the transformation astounded me.
Besides having no hair and being dressed in BDUs (battle
dress uniforms), the guys I had sat with in the Atlanta airport a mere 72 hours before didn't look the same. They actually looked a little more like . . . men.

During daylight hours, our conversation consisted mostly
of a drill sergeant screaming, nose to nose, at recruits. But
we learned how to stand at attention, do (lots of) push-ups,
and "take it" from the sergeants. Experts at eradicating any
self-worth developed in our previous 18 years, the drill sergeants converted a haphazard collection of individuals into
a well-functioning military unit. They strategized, using us

as if merely a life-sized hand of cards in their overall larger game of poker. Having this new identity forced upon us had its benefits. Most of us needed a major attitude adjustment (no one more than me), and we got it.

The first sign that the Army was beginning to have some respect for us came about four weeks into our training. No free time turned into an hour here or there to visit the PX and buy personal items. The respect was not always returned, however. A handful of freedom abusers in my platoon found ways to smuggle cigarettes, chewing tobacco, and booze into the barracks. Movable ceiling tiles provided a readymade place to stash the contraband, but my reaction to the unsanctioned activity surprised me. I recognized a change—yes, for the better—in my own attitude. Back in Kankakee, I would have relished any chance to break rules, especially when it meant liquor would flow freely. My young entrepreneurial spirit might have orchestrated a profit strategy. Now, though, I was invested enough in what the Army was making of me to be apprehensive. I suspected the drill sergeants knew what was going on but were shrewd enough to choose their battles. Yet, I didn't want to cross them.

The lesson in myself fascinated me, and I discovered that if I showed respect to my superiors, they would return the favor. Little by little, I realized that even drill sergeants responded to being treated well. If one of them saw willingness to help or proficiency in a particular skill, they came to count on the reliable ones. Some of us even became "second-in-command," or squad leaders responsible to help maintain order when the sergeants weren't around. Though often it just meant lending us to do the push-ups for someone else's mistake.

Another few weeks in, our freedom expanded to include weekend excursions to nearby Columbus and a chance to see . . . girls! Columbus nightclubs abounded with cute southern ones, and the promise of a weekend with female companionship heightened the discipline among us during the week. No one wanted to be denied a pass. It was a taste of freedom.

One night about 40 days into basic training, I

Prepared for boxing night with Scott Mitchell in the barracks

lay awake on my bunk despite the exhaustion of another day of rifle training, calisthenics, running, and rappelling. Inhabiting a room with four dozen other men, the darkness was hardly silent, but I had learned to screen out snores, coughs, deep breathing, and arguments to focus on my thoughts. That night, the obvious observation that we were all in the Army to learn how to kill other people sparked a deep sense of my own mortality.

I could die.

Early on the drill sergeants almost certainly guaranteed that be our fate. We were 11B after all and considered to them bullet stoppers in the big picture. And to think, we signed up for this. I was only 19, but *it* could happen to me. In my youth others even younger had already experienced that conclusive reality—a reality I knew all too well. The multitude of deaths and deadly experiences was again fresh in my mind. One particular scarring event, and first to memory being, a young girl back in Bradley, Illinois.

Stream of Death

We did what every youngster does when a siren screams nearby: we stopped what we were doing. A bat dropped from the hands of Denny at home plate. Their pitcher, David, turned and stared past the second-to-third base shortstop, toward the tree-lined creek bounding the left outfield. My heart rate jumped as a second siren joined the first, then two, three, maybe five more shrieked in the distance. *There must be six or seven police cars heading to our ball field.*

I squinted past the perimeter as the first pair of red and blue flashing lights screeched to a stop in the outfield. Other boys had begun walking in the direction of the police car, and in the several seconds it took me to collect my thoughts and step off second base to join them, three more police cars, sirens fading, halted by the creek. Before I walked halfway to the crowd, an ambulance joined the police, and eight or ten officers and paramedics scurried around the area, several shouting at someone I couldn't see. Other sirens still whined in the distance.

Boys closer to the scene now seemed to be passing a message from one to another, a wave of agitation spreading toward me with the information. Finally, I heard the words "a girl's body." I stopped and stared at the trees where two policemen were shooing curious ballplayers back toward the infield. The boys, hesitant to miss a firsthand encounter with the mystery, reluctantly retreated, but in a town as small as Bradley, we would soon know all about what they had found in Soldier Creek.

The young girl who had been butchered, wrapped in Styrofoam, and tossed in a tributary of the Kankakee River was only five. Pretty much everyone knew Tara Sue had been missing from home for several days, but no one expected to find her dead. That just didn't happen in Bradley in 1981.

Every boy on the Bank of Bradley minor league team had played in that creek, but the day the police found the Huffman girl in the water, it became haunted. Deep spots revolted us, all fearing another shredded body might surface from the darkness. For me, that day marked the beginning of an intimidating relationship with death. I was fascinated and repulsed at the same time.

A Taste of Religious Freedom

My musings about death continued through basic training but were far less immediate than my musings about how to eke out more personal time in the face of domineering sergeants and merciless drill routines. Then one Sunday night just before lights out, two guys in the next bunks revealed a loophole they had discovered in military life. Apparently, that morning they had gone to church—a right, according to United States law, guaranteed to all American servicemen. Not even drill sergeants could prohibit trainees from attending worship services! Although there was nothing religious about me, I determined that night to exercise my First Amendment rights the very next Sunday.

Why the two I heard it from had not shared the loophole with anyone else, I couldn't figure. I recognized it as an opportunity to enhance my personal popularity and so shared my legal savvy with everybody in the platoon. As a result, the following Sunday at 0700 hours, a formation of freedom-lovers gathered around me at the barracks exit for a mile long trek to the nearest church on the base.

My eyes widened as I stepped into the building, a "sanctuary" as it was then called. Evidently, my guys and I were not the first to discover the church opportunity. In fact, we seemed to be among the last. Hundreds of soldiers jammed the pews. To find a seat in the crowd, it would be every man for himself, and I quickly jostled toward an empty seat in the corner on the back row.

I folded my arms and leaned back in the chair, thankful that, unlike any chair I'd sat in at Ft. Benning during the past six weeks, it was well-padded. Soft notes from the organ signaled the beginning of the worship service. Any remaining tension over the strange new environment drained from my body. I slumped forward, chin on my chest. *Finally*, the thought floated through my brain, *I've found what I wanted.* And slid into a deep sleep.

"Viers!" A slap stung my right temple. "Wake up, man. You just slept through the whole worship service!"

My mind slowly assembled the meaning of the blow and the emphatic whisper. *Wow,* I thought. *An extra hour of sleep! Just what I needed!*

As I staggered toward the exit with my platoon buddies, thoughts came clearer: *this church thing is going to work out pretty well.* I would not miss another opportunity for a Sunday morning nap the rest of my internment at Ft. Benning.

Besides catching up on sleep, I also came to appreciate the liberty of walking to and from church, roaming the streets, free from the shadow of drill sergeants. It was the closest thing to alone time any of us experienced during basic training. The best part for me was that I felt like I was beating the system; I was in control of my "church time."

Several Sundays into exercising our constitutional right to worship, my group arrived early and filed into what had become "our" back row. I had mastered just the right slump to maximize comfort while sleeping, but when I closed my eyes that morning for "my time," the precious glide into unconsciousness alluded me. I sat, eyes closed, chin on chest for a minute. Two minutes. Someone at the front of the church was praying. People around me stood and began singing. For the first time, I was hearing the service, but I couldn't imagine why. I was every bit as worn out from the week of field training as ever. I had just gotten up early, walked just as far, yet I couldn't fall asleep. Why? Something was messing with me.

Another person prayed. More singing. A congregational prayer. Something was said about an offering. Finally, I opened my eyes just as the guys on either side of me handed off a shiny brass dish with money in it. My head flopped back, resting on the back of my chair, and I stared at the ceiling. A voice that sounded familiar began talking. He spoke long enough for me to decide to sit up and watch whoever it was.

After fifteen or twenty minutes, he made an offer to everyone in the audience—something about a free cross, attached to what he called a "Rosary." He had me at "free," so I inched with the crowd to the front of the sanctuary, grabbed my new Rosary, and returned to the barracks to discover yet another level of religious freedom. The drill sergeants weren't permitted to take it from me. I had a right to display in my locker a religious symbol—the only personal item I was allowed, other than paper goods from home.

Since all trainees looked the same, dressed the same, walked the same, talked the same, and owned nothing, I grew deeply fond of that cross. It was *mine*. In the midst of that possession-barren South Georgia land, I discovered how very much I loved to have things of my own.

Chapter 3

OUT OF CONTROL

I had escaped being sent to war, and death. But the past was the past, and I couldn't always shake it. When *they* say youth are impressionable, I would agree.

The murder of Tara Sue Huffman tainted everything about my previously "normal" middle-class upbringing. Friends and I had spent much of our time in typical young-boy fashion—shooting hoops, playing baseball and running around the neighborhood. Then, just a few years after that first encounter with death, came another. This time, on bikes at the Kankakee River State Park, my friends and I stopped in our tracks at the sight of what may have been federal agents. They certainly didn't look like average police officers—or conservation officers either. The scene once again reminded me of the previous episode on the ball field although the urgency and curiosity among the officials in charge differed somehow. We crept through the woods as near to the commotion as possible, hoping to discover the cause of the mysterious on-goings, while crews combed through the thick wooded area about 100 feet from our bike path.

Conversations reverberated back through the official ranks, finally landing on the ears of the curious onlookers. *Telephone cord.* I looked at Darren with a confused look. "Did I just hear *telephone cord*?" He nodded in agreement. So yes, those were the first two clearly audible words I remember hearing. Another couple, a middle-aged husband and his wife, appeared to be on a leisure walk in the park now gathered nearby due to the unusual number of people congregated at the state park. The spectators looked to each other with shrugged shoulders. Police dogs combed the wooded area we had now all presumed to be a crime scene. A moment later what appeared to be a senior ranking officers voice echoed through the barren trees as he spoke into a handset, "Male. Badly decayed. Appears to have been bound with a telephone cord."

The police soon after flushed back the onlookers. We were certain we had stumbled not only on to a crime scene but a murder. We overheard whispers of the discovered remains having been stuffed into a large rotted out tree. Hypotheticals rang out of a mob dumping. Possibly a Chicago hit job and cover-up from months prior. I remember one spectator declaring it "genius", he continued, "It makes perfect sense to dump a body in a state park wooded area in late fall since snow covers their tracks and evidence until late spring and the park reopens." As we peddled away, I could only draw from recent memory the discovery of my last murder scene. Though something about the state park seemed different. The corpse of an unknown man, potentially linked to organized crime, didn't offer up the same sorrow or concerns.

More serious-minded after Tara Sue, and the goon stuffed in the tree trunk, I realized my ambitions soared beyond winning the next sandlot slugfest. I recognized that money would enhance the freedom my parents slowly gave me as I grew and maybe provide some sort of security in a dangerous world. So, I hustled.

I rode my bike all over town, looking for work, and took on conventional childhood jobs like delivering newspapers, mowing yards, and shoveling snow. I discovered, though, that I wasn't just looking for a job. I wanted a *business,* and a local produce store offered my first opportunity. The owner, John Panozzo, never remembered my name, but he paid me ten cents for every flat of flowers I brought out of his greenhouse to the front street area for display. I was in the floral merchandising business! And even before learning to drive, I began following stocks in the *Wall Street Journal.* I understood that money fueled the world, and I set my first goal: to make enough to buy a car when I turned sixteen.

Money-making work became my top priority, followed closely by hanging with friends and flirting with girls. Success as a student ranked far lower on my list of important things to do.

From the combination of having money (and perhaps a bit *too much* freedom), killing time with friends, cultivating my pursuit of girls, and disdaining school, I fashioned a decidedly unhealthy lifestyle. Sometime in our mid-teens, my buddies and I began to have run-ins with the police. It became a form of entertainment through which we got to know many of the local officers. A peculiar bond developed between the lawmen and the lawbreakers (although we preferred to think of ourselves as adventure seekers), and looking back, I believe we drew a sense of security from our relationship—however dysfunctional—with the cops.

They knew our cars, our circle of friends, even what to expect of us on any given night. Many of the same sirens that had broadcast the discovery of Tara Sue's body periodically descended upon the houses where we gathered to drink on nights when adults were gone. And they hauled our collection of underage drinkers to the same jail her murderer, Timothy Buss, had spent his first days of incarceration. We found pride in ourselves on how much trouble we could cause the police, and on a "good" night, the cops needed paddy wagons to cart our crowd of teens downtown for processing. The station clerk knew us well enough to speed through the intake procedure with little hassle. Fingerprints. Calls to parents. Collect a hundred dollars from each kid. It must have been a profitable operation for the Bradley police. Most of us made it a point to have cash in our wallets to pay the "extortion" money on demand. Yet none of it taught us a lesson. Undeterred, we spun through the legal turnstile with binge-drinking, car wrecks, out-of-control fights, and generally disturbing the peace of our little town, and in the later teenage years, once again encountering more than a few deaths.

Business at Last

As a *Wall Street Journal*-reading kid, I had enjoyed watching my profits rise while investing imaginary money in the stock market. If I had real money to invest, I thought, I could strike it rich for sure. So upon returning from Fort Benning as a full-fledged soldier in the Illinois National Guard, I relegated the Army to monthly weekend drills and set about making the money I envisioned to invest, buy, and generally fund as lavish a lifestyle as I could concoct.

"Darren and Brian" worked well together on pick-up jobs in construction during our last couple of years in high school, so creating D&B Insulating was a natural step for us when I returned from Army training. Few other guys would put up with the irritating, scratchy, residue that clogged skin pores daily after installing fiberglass insulation in new homes. To us, that meant there was money to be made, and if no one else wanted it, we surely did.

Although we had no real money to get started, we improvised well. After buying the few required supplies and spending twenty dollars to print business cards, we were on our way. Because we had few competitors, Darren and I figured 1991 would be a good year for us. And while it was good enough to get by on, I was restless for more.

One of my desires in having lots of money was to stabilize myself. High school depravity had given me just enough wisdom to know I could easily run my life into a ditch. So, I sought guidance from people who were leaders in our community. The name I now wanted to make for myself was not the infamous kind my buddies and I had developed with the local police. This time I wanted a good reputation.

I also wanted to stop itching. Darren and I discovered during our "good year" why we were among the few people who wanted the job of insulating houses. It was time to segue from the insulation business. The local Chevrolet dealer played into my transition plan. Working at the service department gave me a great income base, and it also sparked my next business idea.

Strolling through the break room one afternoon, I noticed the vending company rep reloading the machine with candy bars, chips, and gum. *Filling those machines is somebody's business.* In the instant the thought crossed my mind, I knew that some snack and beverage machines somewhere would soon be mine for the filling.

Within a few weeks, I found an opportunity to start small—literally. Gumballs and hard candy provided a low-cost entry into my new market, so servicing accounts became a side gig. As the numbers went up, I realized they were fast approaching the point at which I would no longer need a job at the dealership. And with my Uncle Greg, I spent every evening building a spec house out of steel. It was another great hands-on experience in my early years. Gumballs alone still fell short of my financial expectations, and I still had little working capital—a significant danger to an upstart business—but I filled the gap with enthusiasm for once again being in business for myself. I added snack and beverage machines to my service and then expanded into five-gallon bottled water, leasing coolers to homes and offices and delivering five-gallon bottles to keep them pouring.

I worked long hours but refused to sacrifice my social life for my company. I rationalized a need for both. Shouldn't everyone have a healthy work and play "balance" in life? Yet that thinking cracked open the door to my pre-Army lifestyle, and booze, women, and wild nights rushed in. So much for stability.

The guys I hung out with formed the base for my lifestyle, but women brought the variety. Romances came easy, and so did ending them. A lack-of-commitment gene seemed to trigger in me whenever "things" tipped toward serious relationship. I made sure they didn't go too deep or last too long and always found or crafted an exit from everything that smelled like obligation. The tendency made me an expert at being unreliable for women, so the guys harassed me, claiming that the best thing I could do for a relationship was to leave it. Although I didn't see it coming, my bad habits and risky lifestyle was about to wreck more than just my relationships.

Ditched

I grinned as the speedometer needle on my crimson 1986 Pontiac Fiero crept toward 100, and I toyed with the thought of maxing out the dial. What a great, unseasonably warm day—and now night—January 18, 1992 had turned out to be, even without girls. Drinks had flooded my mob of buddies swarming the indoor-outdoor Chicago Heights Italian Bar. An impromptu bocce ball tournament launched early on Saturday afternoon and continued, under lights, into the night.

Although known for its corruption and connections with crime families since the early 1900s, Chicago Heights felt like a warm, receptive area (or playground away from home) for us. My friends and I relished the tough legacy of chop shops, drugs, prostitution, and the claim to fame that Al Capone started his bootlegging operation here in the 1920s. The infamous figures of those times lured hundreds of young men into a life of excitement and danger, just as gangs do in poverty-stricken areas today. When my friends told firsthand accounts of crime family encounters and chilling, real-life stories of bodies buried in the foundations of old buildings, it sounded like they were describing a movie. The thrill-seeker side of me loved it knowing it coincided with some of the early chapters of my impressionable years.

Although I lived with my mother 30 miles south in Bourbonnais, my friends and I drove north often to party because of loose law enforcement there. The bartender always seemed to forget to check our IDs—an essential key to our fun since we were all underage. And besides, The Bradley

Police needed to move on to the upcoming class of seniors pulling all the same stunts.

Instead of speeding up, after touching the 100 mark, I shrugged and let up on the Fiero's gas pedal. It was probably the only smart thing I did that night. Gathered in the bar's parking lot that afternoon, "the boys" and I had splashed mud and thrown slush balls at each other. By the time we left nearly six hours later, though, we couldn't keep our balance well enough to bend over and pick up the snow. I should have stayed at a friend's house near the bar, but my intoxicated brain ignored the danger of my condition.

Now, racing south on I-57 and still more than ten miles from home, I could barely keep my eyes open. I cracked the window, hoping cold air would keep me awake while the radio blasted something about friends in low places.

The Fiero shuddered from bumper to bumper. My head jerked up and eyes popped open. Then suddenly vibration ceased for an instant as the right tires drifted off grooves in the edge of the pavement. The car trembled again as the left wheels hit grooves, and I glanced at the speedometer. Seventy-two. I jerked the steering wheel toward the traffic lane, but the front wheels had already found snow alongside the road and didn't respond. The Fiero sailed off the embankment.

My body lurched against shoulder harness and seatbelt (maybe I had done one other smart thing in fastening them) as the car, airborne for less than a second, slammed nose-first into a snowdrift-filled ditch and lodged, rear bumper in the air, at a forty-five degree angle. Stunned, I hung in my shoulder harness, staring at the dashboard. The speedometer now read zero. The engine had died, but I hadn't. Nice! I felt pressure on my chest from the safety straps but, as best I could determine, was unhurt.

A thought formed in my brain: *I should be dead.* Now what? At the speed I had been traveling, my life story should have just ended. *God still must not want me. I wonder if He wants to show me a way home?*

I shook my head and began to assess my situation. Thankfully the drifted 18-or-more inches of snow in the ditch was just enough to absorb part of the impact. I popped the handle and shoved open the door with my left elbow. Supporting my weight with my right forearm on the steering wheel, I released the shoulder belt and slipped out into the cold.

Knee-deep in snow, I thought, *How stupid am I? It's after midnight, and I'm miles from home—and probably from any phone.*

Given that I had wrecked along an Interstate highway, another car would probably pass by soon, but I was too afraid it might be the police to hail someone down. Anyone—especially a cop—would smell the beer on my breath, and my experience as an under-age drinker had taught me to take extra precaution to avoid detection. My final situation assessment: I had run my car into a ditch; this would not end well.

I scrambled into a field across the gully from the road and squinted into the starlit night. A white farmhouse to the northwest was the only structure I could see, and a ten-minute trudge through wet snow brought me to the front porch.

A few cars, a truck, and a couple of tractors lined the side yard of the house. *Someone must live here.*

I grabbed the handrail, pulled myself up the steps, and pounded on the front door. A dog barked inside. I pounded harder, intent on waking someone besides the dog. The barking became a frenzy that alerted my drunken self to a new possibility. Here in the boonies, I might not be warmly welcomed in the middle of the night. The business end of a farmer's shotgun could well follow the dog to the door. Not bothering to weigh the other alternative—a kind greeting—I made a quick decision and leapt off the porch. I slid a few feet in the snow, recovered my balance, and sprinted toward the Interstate ditch I had come from a few minutes earlier.

Running increased my ability to think, and I considered options. If I ran south along the Interstate toward home, I would surely be picked up—probably by a state trooper. There are no casual joggers along the highway in the middle of a January night. So, after spotting what looked like the glow of a town in the east, I cut left into a cornfield that appeared to offer the most direct route back to the main road.

At the Interstate, my luck appeared to be holding—no cars in either direction. I dashed across the southbound lanes, scurried into the median strip, then up over the northbound lanes. As I bolted toward the next field, a sharp blow to my midsection sent me flying as something grabbed the front of my blue jeans, and I heard my coat rip just before my shoulders slammed into the ground. Muddy slush exploded with the impact and showered my face with icy slime. I gaped at the sky and gasped for breath.

The thick wool of the now torn coat had saved me from being butchered by a barbwire fence, but my denim pants had been less successful in protecting my knees. In the dim moonlight, I could see bloody flesh entwined with ripped denim curled over my kneecap.

I rubbed my eyes, again amazed at the relative lack of damage to my body after a potentially horrifying collision with barbed wire. Rolling to my feet, I carefully used the fence to stand up. I plodded several steps forward in the mucky earth. More snow had melted here, turning the field into a quagmire. I took a deep breath and broke into a trot, my shoes sinking into several inches of mush with every step.

I squinted and treaded ahead for what felt like miles chasing the light, determined not to run into any more barbed wire, and as I approached the "city," I saw my next barrier and stopped. My heart sank. Through an eight-foot chain link fence topped with strands of barbwire, I could now make out a power plant glistening with lights. This was not going well. There could only be trouble by proceeding this way.

Studying the scene, I spotted a gravel road heading south from the plant. Maybe that would be my first break. It was heading in the right direction. There wouldn't be traffic, and the hard surface would offer better footing than muddy fields. I could stomp the thick mud from my shoes and lighten my load by a few pounds. I estimated the distance to be no more than a quarter of a mile and set off at a jog for the road.

Halfway to my new way home, I stopped at what sounded like the rumble of a truck engine nearby. I stood in the darkness, trying to identify the familiar noise. It was water—lots of water rushing quickly through a narrow channel. I walked slowly forward, staring at the ground in front of me until it ended at the edge of a creek, badly swollen from snowmelt. I looked right, then left. There was no way to the road except across the rushing water.

It looked to be about 15 feet wide and hopefully no more than a foot deep. I formulated a plan: back up for a running start, sprint off the bank, and high step through the wild stream. I pictured my favorite Chicago Bear, Walter Payton, high-stepping over opponents into the end zone. Mustering courage, I retreated a few yards, then bolted toward the water's edge, but my first high step plunged me into very deep, very cold water.

The current swallowed my body. I had badly miscalculated the depth and tumbled, out of control, in the water. Heavy clothing dragged me under as I strained arm and leg muscles, desperately swimming toward the far side. Finding the surface, I pulled myself through the icy water, wondering if I would make it across before succumbing to cold and fatigue. Finally, my fingers touched field grass just as my feet found the creek bank. I grabbed repeatedly, tearing out large clumps of earth and roots, before I gripped two solid handfuls of weeds and slowly extracted myself from the flood.

Disgusted by the feel of a wet wool collar scraping my cheek as I lay beside the stream, my first thought was to dump the soaked coat. But I decided instead to wring it out and wear it. I would need it to regain body heat. This battle was far from over.

I hoped the water hazard was my last obstacle. Once on the road, I paced myself, running a mile, then walking for a few minutes, and then running another mile or so. I felt like a heavyweight fighter after 12 rounds in the ring, but the bell wouldn't ring. And I still feared that the night might end badly.

An hour down my gravel road, I finally came to a landmark I recognized: *Ozinga*. Suddenly, I loved the rock quarry on Illinois Route 50. I was five miles from home. For the first time, I felt sure I would make it. But I needed to rest before the final round.

I scanned the silent quarry, examining construction trailers and heavy equipment. The office trailer would be the best place for a warm nap, but I found it locked. After trying several other storage building and equipment doors, I found an unlocked excavator. Climbing inside, I closed the door and settled into the soft, leather operator's chair. A living room recliner could not have felt any better. Perhaps I would just stay till morning. But an involuntary shudder in my shoulders reminded me of the danger of falling asleep in wet clothing with the ambient temperature well below freezing. If I fell asleep, hypothermia would most likely kill me before the quarry workers arrived later in the morning. So, I pulled the wet wool tight and sat up straight, willing my eyes to stay open for a 15-minute timeout. Then I sucked it up and hit the road again.

This new endurance test evoked memories of Fort Benning, and a cadence erupted from my vocal cords. Singing

focused my effort and reminded me no hill was too high—
or highway too long. Lessons from Army days flooded my
spirit: press on, dig deeper, beat the obstacles; you can do
more than you think possible. Perhaps the misery of basic
training had meaning after all. For the first time, I believed
the lessons from that pit just might serve me for life.

Two hours of self-encouragement brought me to the edge
of town and a pair of headlights wandering in a farm store
parking lot. It was a street sweeper cleaning the area. Still
dark outside, I dashed into the path of the large machine,
waving my arms, unwilling to be ignored. Gears shifted, and
the sweeper rolled to a stop beside me. I knew the company
name and owner but didn't care to share the irrelevant information at the time. I just wanted in. A door swung open, and
the driver leaned out, hollering over the noise of the engine.

"What are you doing?"

"I need a ride home." It was all I could think of to explain
my situation.

The man raised one eyebrow and shrugged. "Okay. But
first, just get in and warm up."

I wasn't surprised that he could see from his perch in the
street sweeper that I was shivering. I could feel my shoulders
and arms shaking as I grabbed the sidebars and climbed the
ladder into the cab.

His name sounded something like "Sam" or "Dan," and
he introduced me to his girlfriend, who was riding shotgun.
I didn't hear the name, or care but I could see compassion in
her eyes as she turned up the heater control and directed the

vents toward me. Sam/Dan said he could get me home as soon as he finished sweeping the parking lot. The thrum of the diesel engine and peaceful warmth of the cab lulled me quickly to sleep. I was back at church in Fort Benning.

By the time I climbed down from the street sweeper, the sky had turned from black to blue to streaked red. I waved a finger of thanks to the equipment cab and turned toward my mother's house. Walking quietly up the concrete steps, I pulled a key from my still-damp pants pocket and unlocked the door.

Stepping inside, I closed the door softly and smiled, grateful to be alive.

Chapter 4

RAT-HOLER

After a few hours' sleep, I roused myself and faced Mom with the news of my ditched car. We arranged for a tow truck, and I rode out to the scene of my wreck. So far, no one—not even the police—had found the vehicle. It was stuck just far enough down the embankment not to be visible from the road.

As the tow driver winched the Fiero up to the shoulder of the road, I shook my head, hardly believing what I saw: virtually no damage to my red friend. The tow driver suggested I try to start it. And when I slid behind the wheel, the car started on the first crank. I paid the driver and headed home, unable to fathom my good fortune.

I went back to "just doing life" until a few years later, fortune showed up in a different form in nearby Joliet. Along the banks of the Des Plaines River, the sparkling Empress Casino and Hotel opened for business.

Taking Down the Empress

"He's not looking very happy."

Mick nodded at the pit boss glowering from behind the dealer at our blackjack table. The suits had joined our action fifteen minutes earlier—about thirty minutes after our winning streak had begun in earnest.

Typically, a bright spring day like this one would find some assortment of Mick, Jeff, Chris, and I at the Kankakee Country Club. In 1994, my roommate, Chris Curtis, and I had found a god to satisfy our restless hearts. A white sphere, just over an inch in diameter, covered with 350 dimples, and named Titleist, the golf ball brought me as much focus and meaning as I could imagine life offering.

My vending and water business had taken off, work at the Chevy dealership was history, and I no longer lived with my mother. The duplex I shared with Chris in Bourbonnais just north of Kankakee had, for a while, provided easy access to my accounts and any social activity I wanted. But what I wanted more than anything was to play golf. That, and my ample free time as a business owner, led to an easy decision: I must join the country club. "The club" was the community's social hub, with the right like-minded people to know in business. The place where business gets done, and in my neck of the woods, only one club would do.

Founded in 1916, the Kankakee Country Club boasted one of the best private golf pedigrees in our part of Illinois. Towering trees lining tight fairways alongside the Kankakee River and a limited roster of members enhanced the stately prestige of the KCC. To seal our connection to the type of life we wanted, Chris and I moved from Bourbonnais to a house on the river just outside the Kankakee city limits but a short boat ride from the club.

Instead of golf, though, the obelisk-gated gamblers palace forty miles northwest of the club somehow called to us that day. Our threesome—Mick, Jeff, and I—opted out of sunlit fairways and into the flashing lights, bells and whistles of the Joliet casino and discovered why we seemed destined to gamble that afternoon.

As we passed the twelve-foot-high concrete pharaohs seated on either side of the casino entrance, we stepped into some kind of a zone. The spring day was warm, but we were hot—*Michael Jordan hot*, I thought.

I split. Jeff doubled down. Mick bet big. We won.

The three of us controlled our table, playing all eight places. From the dealer's perspective, I had the third base side covered, Mick was covering all open spots center, and Jeff had first. We weren't letting anyone ride the coattails of our raging streak. This action was *ours*. But the arrogant attitudes and piles of chips collecting by each of us meant the eyes of the casino were soon on us. Were we cheating? Counting cards? In cahoots with a dealer? Or just simply too darn lucky for our own good?

Thirty minutes into our streak, Jeff, Mick, and I each had our own pit boss scrutinizing every card flip or toss of a chip. The only response to our jabs about beating the house were faces as stony as the pharaohs guarding the casino entrance.

News about a screaming hot trio of players diffused through the Empress, and spectator by spectator, an audience encircled our table. Each time the winning card dropped on one of us, they cheered as if the home team had just won the seventh game of a world series. Even casino waitresses and custodial staff gathered to cheer us on. Applause rippled behind us each time we converted hundred-dollar chips to five hundred, and then five hundred to a thousand. I'd never played behind stacks of money like that. We could hardly comprehend what was happening to us but were only too glad to let the flow—of money and drinks—take us.

I could feel all three pit bosses' eyes every time I slipped a thousand dollars or two of chips into my pocket. At games back home, friends chided me for being a rat-holer, and here in the casino, although not specifically against the rules, it was exceptionally bad form. While hiding chips gave me a safe haven for my winnings, casino bosses also knew that chips not on the table were less likely to be played—and lost.

Alcohol and adrenaline merged to ignite my fantasy life as well. Any minute, I expected the casino manager to invite us into the back room, new high rollers to be courted for more business. Or perhaps I would be a target for a team of floor thieves. I imagined (hoped!) some blonde decoy displaying cleavage would try to distract me while a partner slipped away with a handful of my chips. But neither casino generals nor sexy bandits showed up.

I tossed one last tip to our fourth or fifth dealer—the pit bosses had been changing them so quickly I couldn't recall how many we'd been through, any more than I could count how many drinks I'd downed in the past hour—and caught Mick's eye. He nodded and nudged Jeff. They tossed tips at the dealer, the three of us stood in unison, and we made the ultimate in-your-face move. We scooped up our chips and walked away *before the table turned.*

Jeff, Mick, and I huddled a dozen feet from the stupefied pit bosses to plan our exit strategy. We had no idea how much money we'd won but knew it was more than we wanted to cash in at any one window. Could we manage to get out without triggering the issue of tax forms from the casino? Ridiculous as the notion was—given that we were now the most watched set of players in the building—we decided to try. At least the size of the Empress was in our favor. A gargantuan playroom like this offered dozens of windows to exchange chips for cold, hard cash, and we headed out to try our luck at this next game.

As I stepped away from a second cashier with piles of chips still jammed in my pockets, red lights flashed overhead. Mick, still at the window, froze. Jeff, several steps ahead of me stopped and shot a glance at me over his shoulder as a dozen men in dark suits materialized from among the gaming tables and slot machines to surround us.

Why we thought we could out-smart casino security, I still don't know. No casino will risk an IRS investigation for allowing upwards of $50,000 to walk out in cash, unreported, and we'd been caught trying to make it happen. As bummed as we were to have W-2 forms forced into our hands at the end of our wild run, the "house" did us a favor by catching us before we had done anything blatantly illegal. Better to be nabbed by casino security than the Internal Revenue Service.

I had dodged yet another bullet, but my rush toward worldly success however I could find it simply made me deaf to any deeper meaning my circumstances might hold for me. Taking down the Empress did little more than renew my addiction to adrenaline—and winning.

The Green God

Casino fun was the exception. Golf was the rule. In fact, I had met Mick and his brother Tim at my very first round at the Kankakee Country Club.

A buddy, George Ryan Jr., and I arrived early to spend the day on the course, and my enthusiasm for my first-ever round at the course skyrocketed as George and I decided to look for a couple of victims we could take down for a few bucks in our round. George spotted a cart driven by two men he recognized, and as they approached the ninth tee, we raced to meet them. Mick and Tim Milner, two brothers, maybe in their early forties, had just moved to town from

Fort Lauderdale. In the thirty seconds we spent heading their direction, George had briefed me on the targets. The brothers had sold their radio station in south Florida and bought one in our town. "Good guys," he says.

But our golf match didn't go well—at least for George and me. George had suggested a team match with handicaps: he and I against the Milner boys. We had to guess at my handicap and chose ten. Two hours later, Mick and I shook hands again, but this time I was congratulating the winning team and forking over a hundred dollars. The sparkle in Mick's eye said, "Welcome to the Club, kid."

A hundred dollars still meant a lot to me at that point. As much as I didn't want to admit it, I was far out of my element.

After I healed from our first impromptu match, George, Mick, Tim, and I played together frequently. We discussed business and life strategies, and I learned to appreciate both the importance of new connections and the long-term value of relationships. Through George, the Milners, and others at the club, I discovered how circumstances, events, and people create a meaningful purpose in life. For instance, nearing the end of a round of golf one Saturday morning, Mick shocked me with a question that foreshadowed a great change to come.

"Brian, how would you like to join my wife and me for church tomorrow?"

He might as well have invited me to join him on Saturn. I think I even winced when he said the word "church." No one had ever asked me to go before. Sure, I had led the Fort Benning group to temporary freedom at one, but that was a matter of self-preservation. Why would I *choose* to go some-place like that instead of breakfast at the club and an early start to Sunday golf?

"Nuh-nuh-no thanks," I mumbled.

Back to Golf

Tuesdays and Thursdays I played with the old guys, a special group, but to me, none were more special than Sam Azzarelli. Fifty years my senior, he not only tolerated but seemed to enjoy my friendship and attempts at competition in our afternoon rounds.

Sam and the others in the older set provided my first taste of true leisurely living. Twice a week, we met for lunch, drank and played some low stakes poker, and when the urge hit, we sauntered out to the fairways.

Since Tuesdays and Thursdays comprised only two-sevenths of my golf week, I found plenty of time to keep up play with Mick. Eventually, my social life off the course included Mick *and* Lori. She was a fine wife to Mick and something of a persistent, if not tough-love, friend to me.

Although I could hardly imagine a better life for myself than making tons of money and playing golf every day of the week, Lori could imagine much more on my behalf. The only holes I cared about filling were the eighteen I aimed at with each round of golf, but Lori saw into a hole in my life I didn't know existed and asked me to go to church with her and Mick nearly every time I saw her.

You guys are great people, I thought more than once, *but the last thing I want is to start going to church with you.* After all, Sundays were made for golf.

The Titleist god worked fine for me. I certainly did not need Mick's and Lori's God.

Traipsing through life without a real God is much like wandering through a swamp. You just keep slogging onward. You don't know if you're coming out of it or going deeper in. But you know you can't just stand still. Sometimes you wonder what creatures might be watching from the trees or stalking you from under the water. You slap at mosquito bites on the back of your neck and hope the sting on your calf isn't fatal.

My problem, though, was that I didn't even know I was in a swamp. So I just kept putting one foot in front of the other—thinking I was blissfully happy doing it—but way-deep-down hoping for...*something.* And not-so-deep-down, fearing a bit of what might be *next.* I had dodged many bullets. But how long would it be till my luck ran out?

One thing for sure: I couldn't outlast Lori's persistence. During a Saturday lunch at the club, she finally broke me. I had run out of "other plans" lies to excuse myself from church, and I agreed to meet Mick and Lori the next morning at nine o'clock.

I had expected people like the Milners would attend worship someplace impressive, but Calvary Bible Church met in a modest stone building I guessed to be at least half a century old. At Fort Benning, I had always been able to blend into the background, but here my presence was obvious. Despite

Calvary Bible church where I was first invited to attend.

meeting a flock of obviously nice people, including Pastor Joel, I felt nervous and out of place.

Not a word spoken registered any meaning with me, and I didn't relax until after "it" was over and Mick and I headed to the golf course. In the presence of my dimpled deity, I felt alive to the moment again.

Chapter 5

FLASH BACK TO REALITY

Church with Mick and Lori happened again, now and then, yet golf remained the only partner in life I cared much about. Women came and went. Preaching bounced off my ears. But competition—long drives, chip shots, and miraculous putts, bolstered with generous helpings of liquor, card games, cigars, and of course money—consumed my heart.

But the club did offer some personal growth. Mick and his brother Tim carried on discussions of sales strategy and statistics while playing. Tim and I traded business tapes by leaders like Dale Carnegie and Jim Rohn, and I cherished the knowledge I picked up from the more experienced and savvy men at the club and eagerly incorporated any promising idea into my own business.

My even-older group on Tuesdays and Thursdays also offered a few close and unique individuals I listened to intently. In addition to Sam with his commercial construction and paving company, they included Neil (Jerk) Webber, a trucking magnate, a few prominent attorneys, and Col. Jim Kasler, a P.O.W and triple Air Force Cross winner. Jim also owned South Shore Golf Course, a neighboring public golf club in town and many of our golf and card games consumed a better part of the night there as well. *Tempered Steel*, a biography penned on Kasler's life revealed much more than the quiet man himself. I was taken aback one afternoon when I arrived at the club and received from Jim, a signed hard copy of the novel. He handed it to me without saying a word. (I still cherish that copy and have it displayed in a glass case in my home library.)

The direction life had taken seemed to stabilize a bit from the turbulent past. Everything I needed to know fashioned itself in some form around golf and the connections I had made. I even allowed a little room in my thoughts for Mick and Lori's Jesus, as long as He fit into *my* plans and didn't expect me to relinquish control of my life. Yet on the course, my decisions hadn't always been the wisest, either.

The Storm before the Calm

Summer days ran together, blurring into a simple and agreeable routine. Generally through with my water and coffee deliveries by late morning, I made it to the first tee most days by noon. I often walked 36 holes before nightfall. But the pleasant monotony changed one afternoon in July.

An aggressive breeze attempted to peel the hat from my head as I threw a golf bag over my right shoulder and headed toward the back nine, resolutely ignoring the sight behind me. By the time I reached the eighteenth tee, shadows from the great oaks had dissolved in gray light slowly devouring the golf course.

After hitting a satisfying tee shot to the 175-yard par three, I finally relented and turned to look at the western sky. *Wow*, I thought. The hairs on my arm prickled—whether from fear or static electricity I couldn't quite tell. I clinched my teeth and again turned my back on the swirling mass of charcoal clouds billowing over the front nine. I quickened my pace, moving faster to my ball than my normal 2.5-hour average pace for 18 holes.

Making the turn for the second time now, I teed off on the first hole to start another round. My shot had landed squarely in the fairway. As I approached the ball, set down my carry bag, and grabbed a four-iron, my cell phone bleeped. Mick and David were close and on their way to the club.

"Have you looked up?" I asked, guessing that I would be the only die-hard player foolish enough to challenge this weather. But Mick had had an eye on the weather station's radar and was as determined as I not to let a mere thunderstorm ruin an afternoon of golf.

"No problem," Mick said. We'll make it."

"Right, Mick, I'm sure we have plenty of time. Ha!"

I shook my head, beginning to think both of us might be crazy, and clicked off the phone. Picking up my ball, I slammed the iron back into the bag and double-timed it back toward the first tee—and the approaching storm—to meet the guys.

Five minutes later, three sets of metal-shafted potential lightning rods and accompanying players gathered on the first tee. We glanced at the sky, then at each other, silently agreeing to ignore the potentially lethal clouds now blackening the sky in every direction. Mick teed off first.

By the fourth tee, we began to think we had called the weather's bluff. Perhaps, as so often happened, the worst of Chicago's lake effect storms would sidestep our southern county. By the time we reached the green, though, a blustery chill signaled a sharp drop in temperature. We stopped for a few seconds to watch sheets of rain blowing up the adjacent fairway towards us. Something bad was moving in fast.

Smarter guys would have already taken cover. A half of dozen men from the maintenance and ground crew were already sheltering in the cart barn at the tree line by the fourth tee. As I reached for the flag to let David make the first putt, the world lit up, and a blast of thunder followed even before I could drop the pin to the ground. I shrugged and trotted to my ball, ten feet from the hole. Each of us two-putted, then bolted for the fifth tee.

Off the fifth tee, our drives scattered in different directions. The course lit up again, and we grimaced at the quick roll of thunder. Three of the men in the barn were pointing toward the sky. Two other, gray-haired gentlemen, hands in pockets, just stared us down slowly shaking their heads.

We had to finish just one more hole, and I thought of the

scene from *Caddyshack* in which "the Bishop" golfing in a downpour claims, "The good Lord would never disrupt the best game of my life." A second later, he misses a putt and is struck down by lightning.

Soaked to the skin, I hovered over my sand wedge, convinced that nothing mattered but the game when simultaneous blinding light and deafening thunder nearly knocked me off my feet. A mere eighty yards away, an oak at the end of the fairway, nearest the green, glowed brilliant orange. The lightning hadn't split the course sentinel, but I could hear the sizzle of boiling water. I stared in disbelief at the smoldering oak for what felt like several seconds before it disintegrated in a massive explosion. Steam pressure inside the superheated tree sent splinters of oak in all directions.

"Wow! That was close!" I screamed at Mick and David who were already whooping and hightailing it to the cart barn. Game over!

I charged after them like an Olympian chasing a gold medal. Once in the shelter, we just stared at each other. A whole tree had exploded into mulch right before our eyes—one minute glowing orange, the next nothing left of it but shrapnel. I had been a few feet from near-certain death—again.

Fifteen minutes later, the storm abated, and we finished our round. This time, though, I couldn't shake the sense that something awesome had just happened. Apparently, God still didn't want me, but I did begin to wonder if He was trying to get my attention—either that or He wants me but has bad aim. I tried to make light of the thought but couldn't quite ignore the deeper possibilities. Admittedly, I was getting a bit freaked out by this spiritual stalking.

The Non-Winner's Edge

Over the next few weeks, I began to wonder—to the best of my ability—about life's larger questions. Still, though, none of the thoughts translated into changed behavior. My emotional needs pulled me deeper into the swamp and my focus on accumulating possessions. The drive to "become something in life" overwhelmed the side of me that wanted to stop and think about other ways I might do life. *How long will this run of luck last?* I often wondered. *I better play hard in case it runs out prematurely.*

So, to go with my house on the river, I bought a boat, then a jet ski, and a Corvette. Lori may have been right about the hole, but I just kept throwing *things* into the empty place in my heart. And although each one provided a brief illusion of comfort and contentment, I didn't win at everything.

When I wasn't gambling against a storm electrocuting me, I gambled on my golf and then afterwards in the club's "nineteenth hole" poker games. I usually lost both. The big win at the Empress, though, drove me to find some way to succeed faster than just doing business well each day.

Even though I never paid much attention to football or other pro sports, I began betting *on* sports without *following* sports. It wasn't a smart move, but my compulsion to win sucked me in. And when I heard of people making bundles of cash day-trading stocks via computer, I had to try that, too.

In the glory days of the mid-nineties tech boom, everybody in the bar and clubhouse seemed to be bragging about his or her fortune. They talked often and loud when times were good, but no one ever said much about investments gone bad. Being self-taught in business, I could surely apply those winning principles and learn on the fly.

I tried nearly every tip I heard on sports or stocks, but I was so ignorant at first that when I heard Bulls and Bears discussed at the country club, I thought they were references to local sports teams. I didn't recognize Wall Street jargon, but I jumped in anyway—only to buy high and sell low over and over again. Even those sure thing "inside tips" promised only deeper losses.

My sports results were no better. I bet large sums on games I had no business betting on and then tried even bigger bets to get out of the hole I had dug for myself. What's worse, the bookie didn't like my recklessness any better than the pit bosses at the Empress. My consistent last-minute betting scrambled his books every time I placed money on a game, so I was terror-stricken after a weekend of losses pushed me to the point I couldn't pay my debt. I had hit a new low and had no idea what to do next. Ashamed of the hole I was in, thoughts swirled in my brain but produced few answers.

I pictured one of the grisly, "in the oven you go", scenes from the movie *Goodfellas* the day I met with my bookie to work out a "payment plan." I would be lucky if all I had to do was sell my car in order to pay up. I told him my situation: "I have no money." The ensuing negotiations consisted of a loud, public tongue-lashing in a restaurant full of people. After a barrage of curse words, he granted a conditional release. In lieu of broken fingers or a slit throat—potentials my wild thoughts had concocted—he agreed to accept weekly payments. As his tone softened, I remember the bookie's words trailing off behind me: "And just keep future bets small until you are square."

My inability to pay provided a sufficient shock to my system to stem the tide of my arrogance. With each week's installment, I vowed to myself that I would never again let any vice or compulsive behavior take control of me. "Keep bets small?" No thanks. That racket was over for me. I may be a slow learner with this spiritual stalking thing but the tangible loss of so much money was reality, and I didn't plan to press my luck again.

Chapter 6

911

The vow did a pretty good job of reigning in my gambling compulsions, even limiting my Las Vegas excursions, but it didn't stop me from hanging out with people who still reveled in compulsions of their own. An unseasonably bone-chilling October drove my regular crowd off the golf course and into local bars and restaurants. There we felt the power of being in business for ourselves. The flexible hourly schedules didn't always assist our better judgment. That power of freedom, and being first to arrive at the local watering holes, didn't always work to our advantage.

Porsche 911, patiently waiting curbside

Geared for Trouble

Mike and I had started drinking well before "quittin' time" for most of our community. We had both arrived at T.J. Donlin's early enough for him to zip his new scarlet Porsche 911 into the parking space by the bar's front window. I parked in the back lot. Any red shining 911 in Bourbonnais drew attention in our small town, and we watched and conversed as new arrivals paused to look at the vehicular wonder reflecting the dazzling colors from T.J.'s neon beer signs. Mellowed after our first couple of drinks, we decided the car deserved to be driven, and I wanted to see what it could do.

I quickly steadied myself the best I could after being pinned to the seat while Mike rocketed the Porsche through an illegal U-turn and into traffic. Although accustomed to the power of my Corvettes' engine I was amazed at how this 911 ran in its own league. Across from Olivet Nazarene University, Mike

911 on the wrecker

barely slowed to corner right onto Main Street and began accelerating hard halfway through the turn. Nearing 60 miles per hour mere seconds later, he shifted into second gear. The cool October temps brought with it damp streets, and at that final shift, the rear end let loose, fishtailing wildly. The force slapped us, right, then left, and back again two more times. Rear wheels went airborne, and Mike lost control. We clipped a corner fire hydrant, then roared through an empty auto repair shop parking lot, and crashed into a house. The impact jettisoned us from the car and slammed my body into the side of the house.

For several months, the shift into second gear was the last thing I remembered about our wreck. As my memory returned, though, I relived my body's collision with the house—and then my unreported encounter with a first responder. Dazed and unaware of my situation, I had jumped to my feet and evidently frantically approached the state trooper who had arrived to help. A veteran, high-ranking officer who knew me, he recognized my trauma and tried to calm me down. Unfortunately, he did so by trying to secure my two wrists together. His junior partner saw only the struggle and hastily added to my misery, with a baton which cracked my scapula and opened a gash to the back of my head. Face-planting onto the asphalt lot, I heard Darren, the senior trooper scream, "He's not on drugs. He's in shock! I know him!" And I remember the stitches the younger cop's misjudgment cost me later in the emergency room.

For six months, the scene faded in and out, and I knew my death sentence had been commuted again. Had it not been for the clubbing, I would have walked away nearly unscathed from the Porsche incident. But images of past friends who hadn't been "so lucky" played in my mind again—Greg, killed in a car wreck after signing a minor league ball contract and buried with the Mets jersey he never got to wear in a game; Jason, the prom king, who died that very night of a brain aneurysm

Awaiting my invitation

after the dance; Kris, an acquaintance and party house tenant in Kankakee, being shot in the head at close range by a .22 caliber pistol during a drug deal gone bad on the city's east side. (Kris actually lived.); several suicides, overdose deaths and a handful of other untimely car accidents.

The connections in my business and life has both opened and closed many doors. How they factor into my life's story was yet unclear. I spent the winter recovering in Florida with little to do except reflect, trying to connect the dots in my story. I would later tell Mike, it was his man, and company's street sweeper that had pulled me in and escorted me home several years prior in my Fiero near-death auto escape. But even when

I made it back to Illinois, the broken scapula from the Porsche wreck kept me off the golf course until well into spring.

Confounded into the Kingdom

Since I couldn't yet play golf in April 1996, I succumbed once again to Mick's and Lori's plans for my life. They invited me to an event at Olivet Nazarene University. Although I said I didn't know the speaker when they asked, I certainly knew the venue. The auditorium happened to be across the street from the Porsche event that had almost ended me six months earlier. Perhaps in part because of that, I felt drawn to attend. Lori promised the speaker was business-minded, motivational, and good enough to draw a crowd of thousands. And his talk was free.

Lori had me at "free," especially for something that might profit my business, so Mick, Lori, and I agreed to meet at their house and ride together. We arrived early and mingled at pre-event gathering behind the auditorium. A graduate of the university, Lori knew the faculty well, and as we made small talk with the folks she introduced me to, I heard the speaker's name: Luis Palau. Apparently, the man held something he called "crusades" all over the world. And he had a "Christ-centered mission."

The event was nothing I could have imagined. I assumed the speaker would cover basics of sales and marketing and maybe share a few "never before heard" success stories we could all apply in our lives and businesses. But Palau did none of that. Yet Lori was right. He was motivational—and more.

Every word he spoke seemed directed right at me. I even wondered if Lori had somehow told Palau about me before the speech.

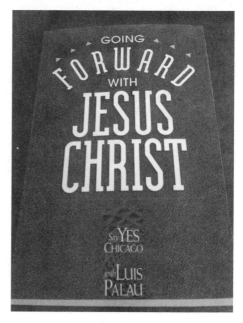

Although I had heard church pastors preach from the Bible, the Palau message was different. He seemed to know what God Himself was thinking as He looked down on us humans—and me in particular. I some-how knew this must be the same God who had been stalking me—and not letting me die—for years. He had "looked down" at the car crashes, stabbings, bar fights, Army training, and assorted other dangerous or shameful situations. And rather than be disgusted with me, this God who, Palau insisted, sees everything and knows everything *still* wanted a relationship. Is that the reason He was so persistent? Could it be that He really does have a purpose for me? Could that be why He never took the hint that I wasn't interested in Him? That I was to play some part in His overall plan for this world? Scary, but I kept listening. I felt Mick and Lori eying me throughout the night, assessing how I absorbed this revelation.

At the end of his message, Palau asked if "the Spirit, through the Word" had spoken to anyone in the audience. Then he invited anyone to come to the stage and "receive Christ" through that same Holy Spirit. I wanted to run out of the place, but Mick was watching me. Sensing my conflict, he asked if I wanted to go up front and offered to walk with me. I surprised myself by saying, "Yes," so Mick took my hand and led me forward like a frightened child.

For the first time since the day at the Empress, I stood before a cheering crowd. Others who came forward seemed less bewildered than I, and despite having just addressed a crowd of several thousand people, Palau himself seemed to sense my confusion. Before leaving the stage, he pulled me aside and handed me a book. I gazed at the cover: *Going Forward with Jesus Christ*, but *I came forward tonight* was all I could think. Palau's name was on the front, and inside the book, I found a yellow scrap of paper offering a few answers to commonly asked questions about a relationship with Jesus.

When I returned to my seat, Mick and Lori smiled and asked how I felt.

"Fine," I said, my face blank.

All the way back to Mick and Lori's house, I felt emotionally drained and strangely vulnerable. It was new territory for me, and I wondered if this family (as Mick and Lori described Christians) required anything more—like attending church regularly or abstaining from some of my favorite indulgences.

Palau had called my experience a "re-birth," and I felt

newly born into a place and way of life I didn't know how to manage. It seemed that I was now a new man. All my sins were forgotten or forgiven or something. Whatever it was Palau had said, I believed him. And I wanted to make whatever life changes I needed in order to "make good" with this new God thing.

Since I didn't know what else to try, I did the only thing I could think of to keep out of trouble. I just stayed home.

Chapter 7

FULL MOON CRAZY

"You've never read *The Great Gatsby*?"

During one of my early nights at home alone, I reflected on a conversation I'd had with a friend I had hung out with a while before the Porsche wreck. She had a degree in journalism and read often.

"What about *The Old Man and the Sea*?"

"No again," I had told her.

The third time she asked about another must-read book I hadn't read, I finally said, "Listen: stop asking me about books. I don't read. Understand? I can't recall ever reading a book cover to cover."

Feeling vulnerable again, that confession was a real conversation stopper. Even in school, the closest I came to reading "the classics" was to watch movies based on great novels. Reading, I thought, was for retired folks.

But as a "born again" guy, everything seemed up for grabs. I felt like I was learning to walk and talk all over—and maybe read, too. My old strengths—self-assurance (a.k.a. arrogance), vision (hyper ambition), assertiveness (unbridled aggression)— would not report for duty under the new regime. So maybe I needed to re-think reading. What else was one to do, at home and bored?

Slow Transformation

Daylight was less dangerous to my spiritual well-being, so I continued to play golf. My friend Sam Azzarelli also offered a new idea in the "hobby" category. A long-time gardener, he allowed me to help with his garden while teaching me to grow and manage vegetables. We even canned our crops together and took them to Florida to enhance meals over the winter. And he shared family recipes for remarkable Italian dishes that I would cook for friends and family for years to come.

But at night, it was alone time. And even though I still didn't do "alone" very well, little by little, I got a handle on the reading thing. I wondered if I might enjoy travel, sports, or business books. Maybe some self-help titles would help me with my business. I was a year deep in a promising expansion into office coffee service and could certainly use a few tips for handling growing pains. Still, none of the usual subjects captured my attention. Then I discovered Sammy the Bull.

I wandered into Barnes and Noble and asked a young staff member if they had any mob books: "You know, the Mafia."

After cautiously looking me up and down, he led me to a section called "True Crime," and I salivated at the thought of reading about the likes of Chicago Heights characters and tales I had heard from friends years ago. Scanning the shelf, a book on display face-out called to me. It was the story of Sammy "the Bull" Gravano. He had turned state witness (some would say "Rat") to bring down New York Mob boss, John Gotti. Sammy had been Gotti's second in command— the *Under Boss*, as declared by the title.

I snatched the book, read the cover, front and back, and wondered how author Peter Maas had come privy to the information he used to write the book. Although not a local crime story, it looked like something I might enjoy, and after twenty minutes in the aisle flipping through the pages, I bought the book.

That night, I read ten pages before falling asleep, then twenty more the next night, and fifty the night after that. Maybe I was a reader after all. My eyes strained at the new and unusual demands placed on them, but on day four I picked it up again, skipped golf, and read for eight hours straight. After that, reading became my new passion.

It was a change that opened the door to other changes, and the new me seemed prompted by God, that Guy-in-the-Sky who had been stalking me for years. And somehow, being home didn't seem quite so alone anymore.

Befriended

One particular change that startled me was my new ability to focus on the serious questions of life. I had no immediate answers about existence and purpose, and while the questions overwhelmed me, I didn't fear facing them—and truly wanted to know the answers. Since "meeting God," I didn't seem to be me anymore. Was He the One truly changing me? Or was I just losing my mind? Random encounters and new connections all seemed to parallel this new theme. Yet, I shared little of these changing concerns with others, feeling confused or maybe even a bit crazy.

Still lodged in my mid-twenties, what would this mean for my future? What would the next 70 years look like? If this is "a foundational period in my life," what am I supposed to do with it? Do I somehow just trust God to take care of me? Or should I use my brain to figure things out? Do I give up control or increase it in the right ways?

I questioned and then questioned some more. I recognized in my wonderings a central issue from early in life: How do I respond to authority? First, it was parents. Then teachers. Cops. Entanglement with a couple of bookies. Now God! He seemed to be the most promising of them all. Could He become not just an authority but a friend to also confide in? Luis Palau had made it sound like that's exactly how it's supposed to be. The process to me seemed more than a *bit* crazy, it bordered on full moon crazy! Who were these new conversations in my head even being directed towards? Or better yet, expect to be answered by?

In trying to understand the changes in myself, I developed a new fascination with observing other people, and my work in sales and traveling gave me the opportunity to meet many unique individuals. And, if my past was any indication, my surroundings always held the key to my future, as if a predestined plan had been written, with each element I encountered having a small part. I talked to people I met about politics, faith, family, and every other "significant" subject I could think of, trying to assemble a God-perspective on the world. Do they feel the same about a "plan for their life"? Do they knowingly participate in a bigger purpose?

Selling became my model for how to change in good ways. A good salesman listens for what's behind the customer's stated needs and desires in order to pick up on the real opportunities—not just for a sale but for a chance to learn, grow, and even teach others later. Salespeople also form relationships. I gleaned some positive relationship principles from that knowledge, but not all relationships—business or personal—are permanent (just ask the girls I'd dated). Some last, but many don't. Which kind was this new relationship with God?

As I paid closer attention to input from my diverse group of friends, I discovered that some of them seemed to have a solid handle on the answer to the relationship-with-God question. They seemed to know a lot *about* God, but they also just seemed to *know Him* on a genuinely personal level.

In one especially memorable conversation, I flat-out asked, "You mean to say you think of God as your friend?"

The answer was a simple, "Yes."

My friend's answer freaked me out, and I exited the discussion without asking any more about it. I may have even wondered if the guy thought a galactic mothership would eventually take him to Mars or some exo-planet.

At some churches, I'd seen Jesus hung at the front of the church, nailed naked to a cross, so this friendship-with-a-dead-God stuff made little sense to me. The God I had "received," though, seemed to be creeping into my life. I even began to see that He may have always been at my side—through wrecks, binge drinking, and other hellacious times—standing by, a quiet, faithful, protective partner. I wondered if I could convince Him to speak a little louder. I definitely needed further persuading. Although some people may have faith in the unknown, I had built an enjoyable life, one hard to turn from without facts. I wanted evidence. True, tangible, hard facts. I wanted that smoking gun, indisputable evidence like the Bourbonnais police had sought out and found the night of the stabbing.

Partly Cloudy with a Chance of God

With winter on the way, I decided I might be able to hear God better in Florida, so I headed south, armed with a library of books and tapes. Since I knew that, whatever came of my "friendship" with God, I needed to keep growing the coffee and water business, my library focused primarily on bettering the business. I was especially anxious to dive into one book that had come highly recommended, and it would be the first one out of the bag once I got to the beachside resort. Perhaps if I could master the principles in the book, I too could become *The Greatest Salesman in the World*.

To my surprise, Og Mandino said little in his book about the kind of sales I had in mind. Yet I wasn't disappointed. The principles of sales and life he outlined captivated me and affirmed my assessment that I needed more change in my life. I thought the book might even be another message from God, but I wondered how I could be sure.

A few days after finishing the Mandino read, I dozed on the beach, enjoying the intermittent warming and cooling of my skin as the sun peeked in and out of drifting clouds, the varying intensity of light registering on my closed eyelids. Thirty minutes or so into my afternoon siesta, I perceived a change in hue of the light and opened my eyes. Gold fire burned at the center of four holes that had opened in the clouds. From the largest opening, broad rays shot under the cloud base, spraying a medley of yellow, orange, and deep purple halfway across the sky. The same stunning bands swept down to the water's surface from the lowest hole and shimmered southward from two smaller holes. I could almost hear the brilliant colors, a visual orchestra playing glorious hymns that God is real. I stared for several minutes at the sight, then jumped to my feet and dashed inside to retrieve my camera. If this were some sort of message from God, I couldn't let it get away from me. *Don't go away*, I thought as I ran to my room. It didn't; my message in cloud and sun stood still as all the other clouds drifted along their way.

For the rest of my days in Florida, I pondered the meaning of this particular visitation. I had read a book that confirmed my need to change. But I wondered if the thoughts it prompted were from God or just me. Then I saw a display of Divine creative power in the sky.

Debating whether to believe there was a connection, I described the sequence to an acquaintance at the resort who went to church regularly, and he told me about several wild-sounding stories from the Bible. Ezekiel had a vision of a wheel inside a wheel embedded with images of strange creatures. Jeremiah saw a boiling pot in the sky. And Zechariah saw a golden lampstand holding seven lamps and a bowl with an olive tree on each side. So maybe my "Electric Light Orchestra" angel in the clouds wasn't so weird by biblical standards. Perhaps such things were real, after all.

Chapter 8

DEVIL INSIDE

I sat in silence for several minutes, hearing only the hum of the refrigerator from the kitchen. Slowly I relaxed my closed eyes and placed my face in my hands. Yes. I know.

I cleared my throat.

"I give up," I said out loud. As best I knew, I was talking to God and had only one thing to say to Him: "You win."

That morning I startled awake in the chilly darkness,[1] I found the key to the change I needed and wanted. I returned from Florida to real winter in Illinois, suspecting that I still had a ways to go toward a steady relationship with God, but life was still cluttered with all the things *I* wanted.

---

1 Recounted in the Prologue of this book.

Although I hadn't been to church with Mick and Lori in years, I remembered that Calvary Bible Church had just built a new building across town in Bradley. Was that the place I feared being late to? And now that I had let God "win," is that where He wanted me to go?

An old phone book revealed Calvary's number. My early morning call was answered by a machine but offered the service times. The first one started at 9:00, so I still had several hours to wash, dry, and iron an acceptable outfit.

Once on the way, my car seemed to be on autopilot. I don't remember planning a route that morning, but I found the church without a single wrong turn. Still feeling thin-blooded from my weeks in Florida, I wanted to avoid any more time in the raw Illinois air than absolutely necessary and parked in the closest spot to the building I could find.

A new beginning for Calvary Bible and myself

I threw open the car door, stepped into the icy wind, and ran for the church. Halfway to the entrance, though, I slowed abruptly, suddenly fearful. *What am I getting myself into here?* I willed my legs to place one foot in front of the other until I stood face to face with a kindly smile.

The greeter at the door appeared to be several decades older than I, but he also seemed genuinely glad to see me. Still the smile I returned for his felt false. What had this stranger discerned about my mental state when I said, "Good morning"? Did my voice and mannerisms signal that I don't belong here? Paranoia engulfed me.

I didn't even know how or where to enter the sanctuary, so shuffled past the man at the door and surveyed the scene for an escape route.

"Good morning!" The voice sounding from nearby, It was Matt Adamson. "Hey Brian" he continued and extended his hand once I turned facing him. I didn't know Matt well but did remember meeting him years past at Calvary's previous location. Thankful for this recollection and not one of past mischief since he headed up the undercover drug unit for the local police department of Kankakee and surrounding areas. Either way I was nervous. I could see he wished to make me feel comfortable coming in but it wasn't working. I wanted to run!

Another voice cut short my getaway plans, and I reached instinctively for the hand extended in my direction. A stranger, but it was a pause I needed,

"Hello." *Do I sound as confused to him as I feel?*

I noticed the man's name tag without reading what it said, but the badge reminded me of another name: *Lori*. If I could just find her, I would be all right.

Matt came close and quietly spoke again before I could locate Lori. "Brian, I'm teaching a class after the service as well if you would like to attend. Its a Bible study on the book of John."

I didn't know John, and wanted no part of it. Even mentioning coffee and donuts. And how I could sit in back and listen while he did all the talking. I thought, no thanks. He sensed the discomfort just before I was able to speak. "I can't breathe." was all I got out.

Just then, the greeter motioned towards the doors, and I could see he was beckoning me toward the sanctuary. The escape I needed. I quickly stepped inside and calmed down enough to regain my breathe. Pastor Joel was already standing on stage. It was the connection I needed. Suddenly, it was okay to be here, and I found a seat a few rows from the back of the large room and nestled in before feeling any further interrogation of my presence unfolded.

For months after that first disheveled Sunday at the new Calvary building, I would rarely miss a service unless I was out of town. Yes. I had changed.

Bedeviled

One night not long after my reunion with Calvary Bible Church, I closed my eyes to pray before going to sleep. This was new to me as well. Sure Pastor Joel prayed at church but now I was at home. What to say? Feeling thankful of late, I mustered the first thoughts that came to mind.

"God, thank You for everything. I don't know what's happening to me, but I hope You are behind it. Thanks for my health and business." As I rambled through a narrative of current events in my life, the significance of this "small talk" with God was suddenly unmistakable. After a few rambling minutes, I heard, "Jesus Christ!"

A deep booming voice startled me fully awake. I hadn't fallen asleep, so I knew I wasn't dreaming.

The piercing interruption morphed into a growl. "Enough already."

I sat bolt upright as goose bumps spread across my arms. Without turning my head, I looked to each side, then at the ceiling and at the floor, making sure I was alone. I was, but I wasn't. Somehow I recognized the snarl as the voice of the devil.

How did he get in my room? Or was it in my head?

Flesh crawling, I barely managed to control my emotions enough to avoid a full-blown freak-out when another thought flashed to mind: *Resist the devil, and he will flee from you.* It must have been a scripture verse I had read or heard at some point. At any rate, it certainly seemed to fit my situation, and in that instant, I understood my place on the vast spiritual battlefield in which every human being is either a victim or a combatant.

The devil is the oppressor of mankind. He horrifies people as a berserk partygoer stabs his friends. I still bore the physical scars of that eruption of spiritual war. Demons do their best work when a maniac butchers an innocent child and throws her bloody remains in a creek alongside a neighborhood ball-field. But perhaps there are also angels—guardian angels, in fact—who become our unseen defenders against enemy attacks, manifested in miraculous escapes. Is that what I had experienced that night in my Fiero?

A scrap of courage returned, and fear became anger, an indignant rage at the pitiless force bent on destroying man-kind. Somewhere in my spirit, I vowed not to be one of the victims. I would be *a fighter.*

"Listen," I commanded back, my voice resonating in the empty room. "I will pray as loud and as long as I want, and I will carry on until I have the final word! If you interrupt me again, I will just start over!"

I scanned the room again, this time turning my head and body to make a full 360-degree inspection. Satisfied that I'd won the battle, I sneered, flopped purposefully onto my back, and squeezed my eyes shut. I thanked God that the voice was gone and drifted off to sleep.

The next Sunday, I decided to test my relationship with Pastor Joel and asked to speak with him for a few minutes after the service. As I told him about the voice in my head, a smile—or was it a smirk?—slowly stretched his features. *Oh, Lord,* I imagined, *he must be thinking he has a nut job in the congregation.*

"Has it happened again?" His response interrupted my paranoid thoughts.

I eyed him for a couple of seconds before answering. He seemed to be taking me seriously.

"No."

The preacher nodded. "Brian, you may find this hard to believe, but I've heard that story many times."

"What?" *Surely he's just toying with me.*

"Yes, I really have." He folded his arms and looked me in the eye. "All I can do is tell you my best guess at what happened."

The man's intensity—and sincerity—impressed me.

"We all know God is real. And we know—because He told us in the Bible—there's a fallen angel named Satan. *He* is also real, and I believe Satan knows you were once his. By your lifestyle, you had pledged allegiance to his ways. But now you've double-crossed him.

"He heard you when you rebuked sin. He knows you've let Christ have the victory in your life. And he just doesn't like that. The voice that night was his one last attempt to keep you from crossing over, away from sin."

Wow. The "crossing over" stuff sounded like Star Wars. *I'd come to the good side, and I sure didn't want to go back.*

On the way home that afternoon, I had the feeling I'd left something unsaid with Pastor Joel, and as I pulled into the driveway, one last question formed in my mind: *Why me?*

The Wanted Guest

Although most days continued to offer freedom for golf and daytime leisure, I had spent a few days too many on a "quick vacation" to Florida after my talk with Pastor Joel, and now, accumulated client needs kept me working long after everyone else had gone home. The clock read 10:30 when I finally slumped into bed. To unwind, I picked up a novel I'd started the previous weekend.

Midway through the second chapter, my eyes slipped shut. Without opening them, I resigned myself to sleep and closed the book. Feeling for the lamp beside my bed, I found the switch and flicked off the light.

Hours later, my eyes popped open. I stared up at the darkness, muscles tense. *Is the voice back?* At the thought, I sat straight up in bed, wide-eyed, heart racing. This time, I knew I was *not* alone.

My eyes drifted to the arched doorway to the hall. Just above the opening, I saw movement. A form softly appeared in the blackness. In that surreal moment, I knew this visitor was one I should welcome and wondered what I should say to the . . . angel. "Hi there" seemed a bit casual, but the being emanated such a gentle spirit, I could tell formality was not required. Before I could finalize my assessment of protocol, though, the angel spoke.

"I'm with you," he (she?) said.

I *felt* the voice more than heard it. In fact, I was quite certain no sound had reached my ears, yet the words were unmistakable. And a message beyond the simple statement filled my heart with comfort, and the visitor disappeared as smoothly as he had arrived.

This certainly isn't religion. My own thoughts took over as I settled back in bed. *Something real is happening to me.*

Ask and Receive

Within days of the angelic visit, I had my first chance to test just how real God's involvement in my life was becoming. At first light, I received "the call" telling me I had better hit the road for a 300-mile trip to see my grandmother for the last time. She had been in the hospital for several weeks with complications from congestive heart failure. Fluid build-up in her body had added nearly 28 pounds to her aging frame, and now it appeared the time had come for God to "want her." My father had come to the hospital from Florida and sat by her side to help monitor her condition. On the phone, he relayed to me the doctor's grim message: "she could go at any moment."

But how could I break free to go? Needing to catch up from the time off in Florida, I couldn't just phone in sick as an employee might do. I was the owner, and my customers depended on me to make up any slack in the delivery schedule.

My heart sank at the thought of losing my grandmother. I routinely charted my winter trek to Florida through her part of Illinois where a couple of nights at her retirement apartments refreshed our relationship. Before the decline in health began that ended in the heart failure episode, we frequented the riverboat casino, (as mere spectators) along the banks of the Ohio River in Metropolis, IL and always dined on smoked barbecue we brought home from Bill's. More recently, I had to settle for enjoying *Wheel of Fortune* with her, and even though my restless twenty-something self could handle only so many episodes, I still treasured the quiet time with her.

I wasn't ready to stop making memories with her, so after a day of consternation over how to handle grandmother and business, I laid it on the line with God. And again I prayed. This time "asking," something I didn't know was allowed. I asked Him to keep my grandmother alive, at least long enough for me to see her again. If it's her time to go, I instructed Him to let her hold on for another 48 hours. That would give me long enough to take care of my customers the following day before heading south to say good-bye. And dad said she may not make it even if I did start driving right away. Still torn, but now satisfied that I had done my part by asking, I slept well that night. It was out of my control.

The next morning, deliveries went smoothly, so my final catching up during the afternoon and evening worked even better than I had anticipated. Home before midnight, I packed a bag and grabbed several hours of sleep before my early morning drive to see Grandma.

The drive down was warm and sunny but seemed much longer than the 314 miles the odometer recorded. My mind wandered through scenarios from a joyous reunion to news of her passing. I was on edge, the unknown knotting my insides.

Walking into hospitals generally conjured unpleasant memories of emergency room visits from stabbings, fights, and car wrecks, but when I stepped through the front doors of small, quiet Metropolis hospital, an unexpected peace flooded my body. Had grandmother actually made it through the night? I shivered at the thought that God might have granted my prayer request.

Following the signs toward her room number, I rounded a corner and recognized her doctor in conversation at the nurses' station. He looked up and appeared to recognize me as well.

"How is she?" I asked, my voice tentative.

He shook his head almost imperceptibly and smiled slightly. With shoulders shrugged, he answered "I'm not sure why, but the fluids suddenly seem to be draining from her lungs and body. She's in her room, eating breakfast."

I could tell he was puzzled by her abrupt, unanticipated recovery, but I knew why. And as if to confirm that God can, any time, do "far more than we can ask or think," Grandma walked out of the hospital that week. In time, she recovered fully and chose to move to Florida. Always the independent woman, she lived alone, but with my father nearby, and I visited her several more years while I was in the sunshine state.

Chapter 9

IT ALL MAKES SENSE

Seeing how clearly God was working in my life inspired me to consider what direction I should take. Og Mandino's story of success had been summed up in ten ancient scrolls. So, after reading *The Greatest Salesman in the World*, I had brainstormed a personal creed for myself, hoping a more disciplined approach to life would keep me headed in the right direction. Was it truly that simple? Just follow a few golden rules and all's well? The creed had slowed me down a bit and set my mind toward understanding my purpose. Now, maintaining the right direction meant more to me than ever, so I pulled out the spiral pad on which I'd written the creed and reviewed how I was doing.

The Creed

1. I wake with enthusiasm at the start of each day.
2. Today I welcome all challenges.
3. I am in control of my own successes.
4. I approach this day with warm thoughts to all who surround me.
5. Nature is being noticed and appreciated.
6. I make a conscious effort to help others.
7. I am taking action to improve my health.
8. I am building new relationships every day without existing relationships going unnoticed.
9. I am confident.
10. These steps are who I am.

Going Golfless

With my new perspective on God, I figured He would be especially pleased with number five, since He's the one who made nature, and with number six, since He'd said in Scripture to "do unto others as you would have them do unto you." Yet, I felt an increasing conviction that something else, not specifically addressed by my creed, needed to happen.

Oddly, the feeling seemed most intense on the golf course, and it drained some of the energy from each round I played. Then, one day, I suddenly *knew*. I found my identity in my golf score. The problem wasn't golf. It was my desire for the country club *lifestyle*! Being there fostered the very worldliness I now wanted to be free from. I needed to refocus my life elsewhere so as to obtain that sense of purpose I was feeling called to—whatever that was.

So I quit. I would have no more sleepless nights due to a poor showing on the course. I resigned from the club and parked my golf clubs in the garage.

Golf took its rightful place in my life, and at least for now, that meant no place. The dimpled god had to be put in perspective since it was truly not a god at all. The real God who had been patiently waiting for me to accept His partnership deserved more attention.

Just to be sure I was on the right track in thinking this way, I, like many new believers, found go-to guys for direction. These older brothers in faith knew the Scriptures well and often gave me verses to study on topics about which I asked questions.

While on the beach, a phone call from Pastor Joel—one of my go-to guys—affirmed that God had placed people like him in my path for good reason. Although I was a willing student, getting accustomed to Christian terminology took some time. If someone were "on fire," I had learned, it meant he or she was excited about Jesus and always ready to tell others about Him. And while I had never thought of myself as a flaming anything, I did recognize my new sense of purpose and a drive to share it. I talked to most everyone I met about my story but was frustrated with my lack of biblical knowledge. Then Pastor Joel called.

My purpose and activity infiltrated many new circles, but it appeared those circles already professed to knowing Christ—so much for my reaching the unreached. As I told Joel about my concerns, he shared a wealth of scriptures with me. One passage, in particular, written by the Apostle Paul, jumped from the page. "I long to see you so that I may impart to you some spiritual gift to make you strong—that is, that you and I may be mutually encouraged by each other's faith." (Romans 1:11-12, NIV).

Through Paul's painful-sounding to help others, I recognized my own need for community with other believers. While a passion to seek those who needed to hear God's Word energized me, I hadn't identified the encouragement that I needed. Personal reflection, reading a lot, and faithfully doing my business was certainly healthy. My interaction with the other believers was spotty, however—usually just when I "felt the need." Pastor Joel's sharing of the verses from Romans spoke directly to my need to "be mutually encouraged by each other's faith" because, as he pointed out, "sometimes those believers also need you." He also mentioned another verse about iron sharpening iron and encouraged me to continue doing just as I had been.

The Return to Golf

After identifying my need for deeper interaction with fellow Christians, I assumed God would want me to spend more time in "churchy" social settings—home Bible studies, prayer meetings, dinner with fellow church members, and the like. Yet I felt an increasing desire to once again . . . play golf.

Hadn't I given that up to find my new purpose? Little by little, though, I realized that through my season of no golf, God had saved me from worshipping the little white god. I was willing to set the sport in its rightful place, and He was willing to use it to accomplish His purposes through me.

Through my coffee business, I began sponsoring events— giving back. Some happened to be local golf outings to raise funds for a particular cause. Could this be how God had in mind to use my fairway and green skills? I actually enjoyed giving more after a day on the links with friends. What a great idea for fundraising, and it seemed everyone was doing it.

Charity play solidified my healthy new perspective on my favorite sport. It was truly just a game, but it could be played with purpose. Instead of a compulsion, it also became plain old good fun. What's more, my game improved! At one local event, I reconnected with Rick. He filled in some details I'd never known about how we first (briefly) connected and why, when I was in high school.

Rummaging through the chaotic assortment of textbooks, gloves, candy bars, and other personal items in my locker, I had stopped as a shadow blocked the dull fluorescent glow over my right shoulder. Two locker doors banged shut simultaneously a few feet away as other students prepped for their next class. I turned slowly, apprehensive about who might be hovering so close behind me.

An older twenty-ish dude with sandy hair stood a couple of feet away. He was enough taller than I to cast the shadow that had gotten my attention. Why had this visitor chosen my locker to haunt before my fourth period class? He wasn't on school staff as far as I know, so who is he?

In 1989, a stranger introduced himself. Rick Selk.

Something about being with Campus Life, Youth, Christ, or whatever that was. That was as far as it went for me. But not for him. He had singled me out as a person in need who also had the personality—and maybe the social status among the kids—to influence other students at Bradley-Bourbonnais Community High School (BBCHS). He wanted me for Christ back then. I had no interest. Nearly two decades later, he finally had me. We were together again for the annual Youth For Christ (YFC) golf fund-raiser at Kankakee Country Club—at the same club I had resigned from years ago after playing hundreds of rounds.

On the morning of the tournament, we talked. Rick wanted to pair me with Jeff Hopper, the guest speaker for the event. He'd flown in the day before from Fresno, California where he headed a ministry called Links Players. Several visionary PGA Tour players had started the organization 30-some years earlier as a way of reaching golf junkies like I had been. Not only did Jeff lead his ministry but he was a pastor and author of the daily devotional *Go for the Green*. And, Jeff was very good golfer. We hit it off in every way. I had questions; he had answers. He'd walked with God for years; I was still learning to crawl with Him. Jeff saw God's hand in everything; I was beginning to grasp the reality of my Silent Partner in life. At the end of our round, Jeff scribbled his name on a copy of his book and wedged it among the clubs in my golf bag.

"That way, you won't forget where you put it." He grinned.

Despite all the other books I'd assembled in my new

library, it was the first devotional I'd ever owned. I was a net-worker and Jeff was a genuine man of his walk. He reached for my hand, and I shook it, knowing that this newfound friend in Christ had already changed my walk with God very much for the better. I expected to follow up someday, but when I did, it was not in any way I would have expected.

Chapter 10

PARTNER UP

"Who do you mean? Me?"

With a mocking smile, my golf pair for the day looked over his right shoulder, then his left, then at me. "Yes, *you*. You're the only other guy in this cart right now."

I eyed him for several seconds, making sure he was serious. "Okay. I'll do it."

I had just agreed to be the guest speaker at Pastor Dave Miller's church in St. Petersburg, Florida and feared I had just made one of the biggest mistakes of my life. *How did I get myself into this?*

The Set-Up

Tournament play for a good cause followed me to Florida a few months after Rick's Youth for Christ benefit when a St. Petersburg area crisis pregnancy center invited me to play in its fundraiser. Since I hadn't played much since the YFC event, the opportunity sounded great to me.

I arrived at the Bayou Golf Club, intent on letting loose and having fun with friends. Before the match started, I warmed up on the driving range and sipped a free beer offered by the beverage cart sponsor. The 80-degree Florida air sure beat the Illinois icebox I had left behind a few weeks earlier, so I didn't know which I would enjoy more—the weather, the golf, or the free food and drinks.

The tournament paired Sam Azzarelli and me with another twosome for a scramble format. As I polished off my beer, two players arrived at the range looking for their teammates. They guessed Sam and I were the guys they wanted and walked over to us.

After introductions around, we made small talk then headed to our starting hole. I spotted the beverage cart and detoured to stock up, in case the beer girl got too busy with other teams to keep us well supplied.

"Do you guys want anything to drink?" I hollered.

"No, we're fine." Teammate Dave spoke for both of them. "Thanks!"

So my party was going solo. Not even Sam was ready to help me with the fun. I rolled my eyes, bummed because drinks always go down better with company. I raised my eyebrows and shrugged playfully at the beer girl, grabbed a few bottles dripping with icy condensation and headed to the cart.

When we arrived at the first tee, play had already started backing up as the tournament non-golfer got lessons from their partners. *I hate slow play.* I fought back irritation. *Oh, well. It's a charity. Just flow with it.*

As we stood on the tee box, I turned to Dave. "So what do you do?"

"I'm a pastor."

I exhaled and feared my party plans were in the final stages of derailment. *I better behave and lighten up on the free alcohol. What kind of microscope will I be under now?* But Dave, the pastor, turned out to be a very normal guy. He didn't seem to care at all about my stash of beer. We found common ground as I mentioned my adventures with church the past several years and how I played in the YFC golf event, as if that put us on an even playing field with God.

The tournament served as introduction to many good times with Dave. A natural sales guy, I had always enjoyed building relationships, but my friendship with Dave provided a benchmark for me to see how my motives were changing. People became less objects for fun, party, and making money and more important for mutual growth in meaningful ways. After all I was still trying to figure out why and how everybody I encountered now seemed to be playing a part in this new motion picture I considered life. Wanting to see what would happen, I attended his church, Faith Presbyterian, a couple of times.

Toward the end of my winter in Florida, Dave and I paired up for a last golf outing at Seminole Country Club before my return to Illinois. During a break after the front nine, he sat quietly in the cart for several seconds, staring in the direction of the tenth tee, then turned to me. At first, I thought I had taken too long. I always consumed enough food for two people while he cautiously monitored his intake.

"I would like to have you come speak to our congregation in December, if you'll be down here."

Planning Not to Fail

By fall, December 11, 2005 felt ominously close. So as not to ruin my summer fun, I had managed to ignore my commitment to speak, but now I needed to transform my panic into a plan. Here I was, slated to speak at some church in Florida I had only attended once or twice. What was I thinking to say "yes" to Dave? For that matter, what was Dave thinking to ask me? And what was God thinking to let me get in this spot? Thankfully, I didn't know anyone, and they didn't know me. *But*, I thought, *I might ruin the lives of some of* His *people*! I had no idea what to say to them and felt like I was in a slow-motion crash. Didn't he remember I was the beer drinking guy when we met? Did that matter in church? I didn't know but, I knew I'd better get help real quick.

One day, I had the presence of mind to pray about my situation, and a name came to mind: Jeff Hopper. Yes, my Links Players buddy—a pastor himself!—would know what to tell me. So I emailed him later that day.

Jeff and I talked and emailed several times about my December engagement, walking me through how to develop a speaking plan and deliver a focused message. It helped tremendously. But the most encouraging and calming advice he gave me was to trust that the passion God transfers through me is more valuable that any specific words I could add to what His Word already says. Comforted by those words, I knew I could go with that.

What I didn't know was how terrified I would still feel as I stepped up on the platform and walked to the podium. Dave's introduction bounced off my numb ears. And as if I needed additional concern, the place was packed. It was their Christmas cantata which accounted for several dozen of the church's orchestra and choir members standing in formation and on platforms directly behind me. Approaching with a feeling of nervous arrows hitting me from all directions, I heard only enough to know when I should stand up. As I settled behind the podium, my mouth was so dry I wondered if I would be able to part my lips and speak. *God, You better help me, or I'm going down with the ship.* I looked at the faces in the pews and swallowed hard. *Remember everything happens for a reason, don't stare at any one person, scan the room, and stay calm.*

Exhale. I stood taller, making eye contact with a couple of nodding heads which seemed to offer a vote of confidence—all the extra support I needed. I rested my notes on the podium and opened with a prayer. Words came out. It felt like me talking. Something I said triggered laughter in the audience. I talked some more and really meant whatever I said. Smiles, formed and at times, tears flowed on a host of faces in the congregation. By the time my no-longer-dry lips stopped moving, I realized that I had connected with the people "out there" just as Jeff said I would. As I stepped down, someone handed me the notes I had forgotten to use.

California Calling

A few friends from town had also caught the sunshine and opportunity bug after high-school and drifted out to Los Angeles. So to my days in Florida, I added frequent trips to California to sample the winter warmth there.

Three months after speaking in St. Petersburg, Jeff Hopper had phoned and asked me to visit Fresno. A ministry board meeting and golf weekend would be taking place and I could join in the fun. It sounded great. I could time it with an L.A. trip and drive north for some golf, no problem.

But that weekend was an eye opener. The men on the ministry board for Links Players were all wonderful to spend time with. As I had done before at the club, I relished the opportunity to listen to voices other than my own. These men, many much older than I, also flew in from around the country and each was well established in business or profession. I enjoyed the learning, laughter and most importantly the focus on serving Christ. It was all new to me.

A couple of weeks after my Fresno trip, I received a call from Jeff, this time asking me to become a board member for Link Players Ministry. Relishing the opportunity to take part in something bigger than myself (and a golf ministry no less!), I jumped at the chance.

What a remarkable path I'd been on! An unknown Silent Partner at one point convinced me to leave a game I loved to make sure it wasn't more important to me than He was. Then He brought me back to golf with a purpose—first as a fundraiser, then the Links Players ministry to establish Bible study groups in private clubs all over America. I began to see what serving God was about, and I began to look for others.

God must have been looking for opportunities for me, too. After a road trip from Fresno back to Los Angeles before flying home, I pulled into my favorite outdoor café, ordered my usual black cup of coffee, grabbed a pad of paper from my briefcase, and started to . . . write. It became a devotional, threaded with God's Word, and insights I'd learned from the game of golf. The trip and recent round of golf there had also taught me a valuable lesson about not giving up. Something I felt needed to be captured while fresh in my mind. "Perseverance" I would title it.

Months later, thanks to Jeff's amazing editorial work, he published the devotional online through Links Players. After that, I contributed monthly devotionals for the ministry. With each devotion, I re-taught myself whatever lesson I wrote about. After all I'd been through, the first one was especially poignant on perseverance, so I figured the works would be eye opening for me. I realized, I had always found a way to grow through dire circumstances. As I matured in faith and discovered Who was beside me, I learned obedience and trust that encouraged even more perseverance. More often than I liked to admit, the hardest part of the journey was to be patient and relinquish the reins.

LINKS DAILY DEVOTIONAL

A ministry of Links Players International

PERSEVERANCE

"Consider it pure joy my brothers, whenever you face trials of many kinds, because you know that the testing of your faith develops perseverance." (James 1:2-3 NIV)

An unfamiliar golf course, temperatures barely reaching the mid-50s, light winds and scattered showers are what we faced that recent chilly April morning.

The fairways were saturated from several days' rainfall, lengthening the course as well as slowing the greens considerably. Water hazards grew to exaggeration and appeared in places never before in play.

With acceptance of the circumstances and adjustments having been made, I found myself 1-under par after the front nine. I had stood my ground, persevered and felt as if I was in control of my game.

How soon change appears in our lives!

On the tenth hole, after a fine drive in the middle of the fairway, my 7- iron caught up in the wind and came up just short with a front pin placement. The pitch came off the face strong and ran well past. Missing the putt, I made bogey.

My mind now in the way of my swing, the downward slide began. I had lost all focus and was unable to play any shot with confidence or execution on the remaining holes.

My confidence had obviously left my golf game--yet comfort in my walk with Christ strengthened me (a far cry from the old days!).

I was able to smile on the inside, knowing I was passing the testing of my faith and not allowing this silly game we call golf to dampen what really matters: our relationship with Christ and others and how we truly persevere when being tested.

As Christians we will continue to be tested on and off the golf course. Life will throw challenges our way. Persevere and be encouraged in faith during such difficult times!

Even though the swing and back nine score had unexplainable flaws and even led to an almost record high number of sha--s (can't say that word!) on the course, I grew from the experience and enjoyed the fellowship with my playing partner.

I can relate to James in 1:12 when the apostle stated, "Blessed is the man who perseveres under trial, because when he has stood the test, he will receive the crown of life that God has promised to those who love him."

Today look beyond the difficulties you may be facing and toward "the crown of life."

Chapter 11

BLINDED BY THE LIGHT

Years of wintering at the beach made Florida feel like my second home. The day I met "Tony," though, nearly elevated its status from second to first; he could have walked out of the Chicago underground.

Friendship Brewing

Three hours in the poolside sun was not sufficient to prevent a chill running up my spine as a man large enough to be a world-champion wrestler marched toward me, his dark, emotionless eyes staring through my face. *This feels too much like the bad side of home. . . What is that in his hands?*

Evidently, my earlier encounters from a distance hadn't been enough to keep a comfortable space between me and this thuggish creature. I had seen him from time to time through the years and never wanted to be closer than across the room from him.

From a safe distance, I had heard his accent and imagined him to be a Russian version of Tony Soprano. At best, he reminded me of a bocce ball buddy from the dark side. And now here he was, making a beeline for me from the other side of the pool. I had something like fifteen seconds to size up his game. Did he figure me for some sort of competitor? What "deals" could he possibly think are going down at a beach side resort in St. Petersburg? Was this somehow about his wife? He noticed I'm single, and she might need protection? Panicked assessments whirled in my brain, and then I identified the object he carried toward our confrontation. It was a *casserole dish*. Death by casserole dish seemed highly unlikely.

Tony stopped beside a small table at the foot of my beach chair. Face still expressionless, he set down the pot.

"Shoop."

I translated the mumbled word as "soup." He seemed to be trying to communicate.

I tensed again as his right hand reached into a bag he held under his left arm. The tanned burly man extracted a 16-ounce hot-foods Dixie cup, picked up the dish, and poured me a serving of steaming liquid. It was nearly one o'clock, and since I hadn't eaten breakfast, I was starving. It smelled delicious and appeared to be homemade.

My usual beach-day diet consisted of Cuban sandwiches or any Italian item from the menu at "Original Pizza," a friend's place just down the beach whose family and Sam Azzarelli's family were from the same small town in Sicily. I think Sam enjoyed that known connection with their families and much as the food so we would regularly patronize the place. (Besides, that was the way things were done where they come from—doing business with a fellow Paesan). As hungry as I was, certainly Tony's soup would hit the spot, and there would be plenty of other days to grab a local meal.

Tony fished a plastic spoon, cup lid, and napkin from the bag under his arm. He seemed intent on providing full service. *Is he also going to tuck a bib in my shirt?*

He handed me the soup and nodded. I slurped a spoonful and wondered what I should say to this stranger whose food I was eating.

"Are you here for the month or all winter?"

"No, it from can," he says.

Perhaps a bit of miscommunication. I understood, though, that the soup wasn't homemade after all, but it was delicious all the same. I tossed him an approving nod and a smile. He nodded, turned, and retraced his steps to the other side of the pool and into the hotel.

I stared after him for a minute or so. *Did I just make a new friend?* I chuckled at the thought of "friendship" with a Tony Soprano. *I should probably return the favor somehow.*

The next day in the hotel atrium, I spotted Tony standing just outside the exit to the pool. I had come prepared to keep the gift-giving in balance and crossed the lobby. I pushed open the door and handed him a pound of coffee. Traveling with spare bags of the world's most popular hot beverage had become a recent outgrowth of the office coffee service side of my business. Nothing initiates relationships, I found, quite as effectively as a gift of coffee.

Tony looked at the package in my extended hand, smiled warmly and grunted, "Give to me wife." I followed his finger, pointing to a woman lying in the sun by herself on the other side of the pool and chatting on a cell phone. *This blows my jealousy theory out of the water.*

I strolled over and handed her the bag. She stopped talking but didn't reach for the coffee, her eyes questioning. I pointed back toward Tony as if to say, "He told me to give it to you." She looked from the bag, to my finger, then at Tony who was nodding. As if she had learned well the proper response, Tony's wife also nodded and took the bag from my hand. Glad that I did not have to engage the woman in conversation, I walked quickly away and commandeered a chair on the far side of the pool.

Even though my encounters with Tony turned out to be harmless, they had elevated my anxiety level, and I wanted nothing more than to doze off in my chair and let the coffee delivery to his wife be the end of our relationship. For the next hour or so, I drifted in and out of sleep, lazily wondering about the "setup" of those encounters. Maybe I needed to lose my rough edge, to care more about the people I see from day to day.

I drew no firm conclusions about the purpose of my interaction with Tony, but later, back in my room, I realized it was

New Year's Eve, and I was alone at the beach in Florida. Yes, my life was changing; I would never have let that happen before.

A loud knock at the door startled me from my thoughts. *Maybe I won't be alone for New Year's after all.*

I squinted through the peephole, then stepped back from the door. I couldn't believe what I saw just outside my room. It was Tony's son. *Son of Tony,* I thought for dramatic effect. *Is he here to finish the business? To finish me?*

I took a deep breath and turned the door knob. The young man was tall enough to look me in the eye, but when I forced a smile at him, he glanced nervously at the floor. He said nothing for several seconds, then looked at me and spoke without an accent, "Thanks again for the coffee. Here's some grilled chicken and steak with bread. Good-night." Without waiting for a reply after handing me the food, he turned and half scampered down the hall.

Whether the meal was from a box, a can, or an assortment of handcrafted ingredients I couldn't tell, but the savory food left me pondering the meaning of the Tony encounters once again. The Bible speaks of grace as "unmerited favor," and that seemed to be what I received from Tony. He simply gave me a gift with no assumption that I would return the kindness.

I paused in my thoughts to thank God for the grace He had shown me. On my own reckless journey, I shouldn't have lived past my twentieth birthday, but now a new life of spiritual and physical blessings continued to open for me. What a strange messenger of grace I had met here at the resort. A man I dreaded meeting taught me about kindness I should learn to share with others. So often, I realized, I don't understand the route God takes me in life, but I do know now that His ways are higher—and much wiser!—than mine. Connections matter.

Chapter 12

SERVING LOUD AND CLEAR

At a Tampa Bay Buccaneers game many years ago, Sam Azzarelli introduced me to his brother, Bart. Several hours before kickoff, we joined him at a private parking lot directly across the street from the stadium. A sign on the entrance gate read, "Azzarelli Parking Only" *Talk about a convenient location!* Brilliant sunshine and crystal blue sky defined a perfect game day and for me, an incredible introduction to the new Tampa Bay stadium.

Open trunks and rear hatches created a forest of good times for football fans. Sam, Bart, and I did our part by grilling Italian sausage and imbibing a generous sampling of drinks before the game began. With a little less than an hour to go, we packed leftovers into Bart's cooler and headed into the stadium. As the Buccaneer's pirate ship hovering above the end zone seats boomed an opening volley from its celebration cannons, we settled into Sam's 50-yard-line seats a half-dozen rows up from the field.

It was the first of many cannon blasts on a wildly successful day for Tampa Bay. Victory appeared certain when, a few minutes into the third quarter, Sam asked if I would like to go up to the skybox. I simply gave a look to say, "Why would I *not* want to go up to the skybox?"

Sam spoke for his brother and explained that his nephew, Bart Jr., owns a skybox and had a group of people up there. He pointed over his shoulder in the direction of the premium seating. I followed his finger and could make out a group of people standing behind a plate glass window about hundred feet above us. As we stood to leave, Sam offered a disclaimer about life in Bart Junior's skybox.

"He doesn't allow alcohol up there." Sam raised his eyebrows. "He's really religious. Born again, you know. Even has the saying 'Jesus is the water of life' displayed on the sides of his construction trucks."

I shrugged. "I guess that's okay."

I could certainly follow Bart's rules in exchange for a visit to the skybox. Sam and I had a remarkable time with Bart, Jr. and his friends that day—a remarkable time that I repeated with Bart, Jr. six months later when he showed up at the Kankakee Country Club. In town to visit family, he quickly remembered our winning game day and insisted on spending some time together. He drank in the details of my spiritual journey advancement and then a cup of coffee or two. I was excited to have an ear to share what the past several months had done in my life—and of course left him with a few pounds of Viers Coffee to take home.

Serving More Than Coffee

Does God use the likes of golf, family, football, and business...by design? I think He does exactly that. He created and owns the whole universe, so it is natural that He would weave our lives together however He wants.

Over the years, I've watched the pieces of my life converge or at times collide. The spiritual conversion and astounding personal changes and convictions in me are so great that I still can't fully comprehend what God has done. The changes made me want to serve the Silent Partner I had resisted for so long, and as was my pattern in business and life, I learned from other people who were already doing what I wanted to do. By example and some coaching, they taught me what to do (and not to do) in my efforts to follow God.

Bart, Jr. was one of the people I watched. I watched the way he ran his company in Tampa, and I watched him serve God through the way he did business. Giving back not only monetarily, but he also shares his faith with people he meets in the course of working each day. Soon I would learn to do the same.

I didn't realize that giving coffee as a "peace offering" to "Tony Soprano" set the stage for a long term personal ministry. I deliver coffee to businesses every day, and now at opportune moments, I give it away, pound by pound, as a door-opener to relationship. It's a natural outflow of who I am.

Since I downed my first cup of black coffee at the Chevrolet dealership service counter, my life has been built around "the cup"—and so are many inspiring images from the Bible. In Scripture, a cup represents experiences that are to be endured. Jesus said, "O My Father, if it is possible, let this cup pass from Me" (Matthew 26:39, NASB).

"The cup" also refers to the blessings of God. In Psalm 23, David rejoices in the favor of His God: "You prepare a feast for me in the presence of my enemies. You honor me by anointing my head with oil. My cup overflows with blessings" (Psalm 23: 5, NLT).

In a humble way, I intend that my work adds to the blessing version of the cup. Each of our business cards, trucks, product packaging, and our corporate mission statement include two key concepts about what we do. One is this verse: "Trust in the Lord with all your heart and lean not on your own understanding; in all your ways submit to him, and he will make your paths straight" (Proverbs 3:5-6, NIV). The other is my business slogan: "Serving More Than Coffee."

Now I realize, the people, places, and things I have encountered have become the platform I am to serve. I am where I am for a reason. Circumstances good and bad have been an enlightening, growth process—a process I once believed I controlled.

Chapter 13

BE BOLD

No one has ever seen God.[2]

That sweeping statement about the collective inability of mankind throughout history to apprehend God visually has caused problems for virtually every human being who has ever lived. A few have concluded that God simply doesn't exist. Others have left room for the possibility but assume He has nothing much to say to anyone. Some suppose God is around somewhere but disdain Him for keeping so much to Himself. But there are also those who have learned that a visual encounter with an Almighty God is not the only possible evidence for His existence. Even

2 John 1:18 (HCSB).

more, they think He is dramatically and wonderfully part of the individuals who care to discern His presence.

The idea of some great power working incognito among us is not an outlandish notion. Growing up and young in business there was always just a bit more going on than simply what meets the eye. As I said earlier, connections matter. Local coffee shop patrons could fill your ear with what they know but probably wouldn't dare tell about why a few recently-awarded major construction contracts or government contracts ended up the way they did. In Illinois politics since Al Capone first drew attention to the Southside of Chicago nearly a century ago, money is power, and around here, it quietly makes things happen that might otherwise happen a little differently. Small towns sometimes stay small for a reason—business as usual, when the right people are taken care of.

I've been an entrepreneur for nearly thirty years and have seen countless instances where a person of financial means stands behind someone putting "sweat equity" into a business in order to make the venture possible. And truth is, I've been the recipient on several early ventures, but despite my reference to the darker side of Chicagoland, most such relationships are completely legit. In fact, they're crucial to American business.

So if it's readily accepted that someone behind the scenes is "pulling the strings" to make business operate the way it does, why is it so difficult for us to accept that on a much more meaningful scale—the very purpose of our existence—things are caused to happen by more than what seems obvious on the surface. We may not see "with our own two eyes" the way power in the spiritual realm changes hands and moves events to a pre-determined conclusion. But the evidence suggests that is exactly what's happening, and the signs come at us in abundance if we are willing to acknowledge the patterns in play.

After starting my first business while still in my teens, I frequently did not feel very much in charge of what happened to me, but neither did I think anyone else was. Why would there be any more at work than what meets the eye? It's an odd perspective for someone as aware as I was of the people so often making things happen behind the scenes in business and government, but opening my eyes to more was a long time in coming. One particular encounter with a set of signs offers a final perspective on how this happens in life.

Signing Your Life Away

Warm sea-scented air washed in the open window as I steered my rental car toward the St. Petersburg sailing center and marina. I sipped my second cup of French roast from the stainless-steel travel mug I had just received in exchange for a recent gift to the ministry of World Vision. *What could be better than this?* Nothing, I was quite sure.

I turned into the rising sun perched over Central Avenue and felt a deep connection with God's beautiful world. People were already up and active. Runners and cyclists roamed the streets in packs. As I crossed the charming two-lane wooden bridge toward a majestic morning sun, it's assortment of colors framed the entrance for the sailing center. Masts rocked gently in seemingly endless rows of sailing vessels of every size while morning sun shimmered on the water between piers and docks.

Enthralled by the scene, I did not at first see the unfamiliar signage lining the roadway. When I did notice, I checked my rearview mirror, saw several behind me, and wondered how I could have missed them. The creativity and color of the new signs had obviously been designed and produced at great expense. *Nice touch*, I thought. *I guess things change in nine months.*

I pulled into my usual spot at the marina office and stretched out of the car into the perfect day. Strolling up the sidewalk, I sniffed the salted air and loved it as much as always. I scanned the pier, looking for boats for sale, ever hopeful of finding an uncared for or abandoned boat offering a great deal and bringing me one step closer to permanent living in this warm and wonderful place.

Still eying the boats, I tugged at the office door. It didn't open. I pulled harder. After jerking the handle several times, I accepted my fate. The door was locked. Then I saw the too-big-to-miss note I had missed: WE HAVE MOVED.

I stared at the note, confused, then turned back to my car. *Moved where?* I wondered.

I opened the sunroof as I pulled out of the parking lot to retrace my steps. There were the beautiful new signs again.

Suddenly, I recognized the larger purpose to the beauty

of the signage. They had a message I had missed in my earlier self-assurance that I knew where to go. They had the answer to my question, "Moved where?" Each one said:

MARINA OFFICE THIS WAY

Simple enough, but I had ignored the meaning of the signs I saw on my way to the marina. They were there—with the message—but I hadn't known what they meant.

That's when I realized how often I had walked through life without discerning the many signs God placed along the way for me. He certainly did not want me to die all those times when I "should" have, but just as certainly, He did *want* me. I was the one who didn't want Him. Yet He continued to pursue me, guiding me and protecting me—opening the right doors, closing the wrong ones. Everything orchestrated in His timely fashion, those dots I forever tried to connect finally making sense.

I also recognized that this truth is not just for me. Signs abound everywhere and for everyone. The Apostle Paul wrote in Romans 1:20, "For since the creation of the world God's invisible qualities—his eternal power and divine nature—have been clearly seen, being understood from what has been made, so that people are without excuse" (NIV).

For me, the signs were sometimes subtle. At other times, they were sledgehammers—like an exploding tree on a golf course, driving into a ditch at 70 miles an hour, or even a late night wake up call from a heavenly messenger. Often, I considered whether or not I was looking at a sign, but I almost always missed God's message. Still, as Paul noted, I was "without excuse."

If you've wondered whether or not you may be seeing signs in your life, I can fairly well guarantee that you have. Many of those signs are in nature. Perhaps you've marveled, like I did on the beach, at a seemingly angelic visitation in the clouds. Or maybe you've endured hard times—a cup of difficulty—you don't understand. If so, it's likely time for a "gut check" to find out exactly what they mean. As in business—legit and not so legit—many crucial things happen behind the scenes to put the profit picture together. In life, as I said, it works the same way. And chances are the Silent Partner is waiting to connect up with you, too.

AFTERWORD

The process in which this compilation came together does not fit a standard timeline. It doesn't offer a fairy tale ending. And in no way is it meant to sway the readers conviction based solely on my dramatic experiences or beliefs. What I do hope and pray though is that what has happened in your life, the people you encounter and your personal experiences begin to shed light on a bigger picture. A narrative set in your youth as it had been in mine. How significant that process is in all of us. Shaping each of us.

I thank you for taking the time to read my story and ask that if it impacted you or you know someone that could use a little hope in their life, that you would share it.

Sometimes we all just need a little commonality, someone to relate to. Belief is bigger than all of us!

May God guide and bless the path you are on,
Brian

SERVING MORE THAN COFFEE

BRIAN L. VIERS

Stay tuned for Brian's next book—
*"Serving More Than Coffee, **True** Success"*
ISBN 978-0-9996072-1-3

vierscoffee.com